I0820874

MYSTICAL MOCKTAILS

60 Nonalcoholic Mindful Recipes, Rituals, and Affirmations

Julia Halina Hadas

AMBER LOTUS®

The authorised representative in the EEA is Simon and Schuster Netherlands BV, Herculesplein 96 3584 AA Utrecht, Netherlands. (info@simonandschuster.nl)

Amber Lotus
an imprint of Andrews McMeel Publishing
a division of Andrews McMeel Universal
1130 Walnut Street, Kansas City, Missouri 64106

www.amberlotus.com

26 27 28 29 30 RLP 10 9 8 7 6 5 4 3 2 1

ISBN: 979-8-8816-0339-7

Library of Congress Control Number: 2025941034

Editor: Katie Gould
Art Director: Brittany Lee
Production Editor: Brianna Westervelt
Production Manager: Tamara Haus

CONTENTS

EEN of CUPS.

FOREWORD

We all have our own mocktail journey. These nonalcoholic beverages offer a way to enjoy the same sophistication and complex flavors of a cocktail but without the alcohol. For some, it might be taking a break from alcohol for "Dry January." Others might enjoy an occasional drink or abstain from alcohol altogether. There's a variety of reasons someone might not drink—medical concerns, pregnancy, sobriety. Perhaps they simply don't want to drink. And honestly, they don't need a reason at all. There should be options for everyone at the table.

Growing up, I never saw my mother drink a drop of alcohol, a stark contrast to my Polish father, who smuggled high-proof vodka from his home country. Before I was even of legal drinking age, the metaphysical shop I did energy work and readings at held AA meetings in the back. Many of my coworkers were sober or preferred to drink only on occasion. So when I got into bartending, I learned to craft nonalcoholic versions to share. Because at their core, drinks are about connection—connection with loved ones, yourself, the universe, or even an intention.

Especially as I get older, I crave more low- and no-alcohol options. Some of you might be like me—drinking on occasion or seeking low alcohol by volume (ABV) options. You might be like my mother, who mostly abstains from alcohol, except on the rare occurrence. Others might be like my partner, who is sober. There's a rainbow of ways people drink and enjoy beverages. But regardless of reason, there should be options for everyone. When your drinks become about the meaning and ingredients behind them and you remove the alcohol, you open yourself up to limitless creative and healing magic. I hope you find that within these pages.

FILLING UP YOUR CUP

The cup is both a physical and spiritual vessel: It holds sustenance through which we nurture our wellbeing. It's symbolic of what we allow in our lives, whether your cup is full or empty, whether it is stagnant or overflows. It is a metaphor for how we nourish ourselves and the energy we allow into our body, our life, and even the energy we share with others—you can't pour from an empty cup.

What do *you* fill your cup with? Is it something that nurtures and sustains you? With the modern mocktail movement, this is a question many people are asking themselves. While many feel alcohol is so ingrained in our culture despite its negative aftereffects, they crave the connection that often happens around the cocktail and are looking for healthier, intentional alternatives. Mocktails are a reminder to enjoy not just good drinks but ones that nurture your body. And when made magically, your mind and spirit as well.

What if instead of an ordinary mocktail, you had one that matched what you're working on in life right now? For example, a drink for positivity or confidence? One for letting go and releasing? Or remembering loved ones? By incorporating the folkloric meanings and energy behind your drink's ingredients, you can come into alignment with your goals and have the perfect recipe for every occasion.

Think of this practice as a way to make your drinks meaningful and become more mindful of what you sip. When you make what's in your cup magical—aligned with an intention—it becomes a potion and a symbol for what you're bringing into your life. Nurturing beverages have the potential not just to uplift the spirit but to change your energy.

INTRODUCTION

Mocktails are healing.

Yes, the mocktail movement is in large part due to rising health consciousness. The zero-proof and free-spirit movement has marked a shift in focus to replenishing the body and mind. It has shed light on how the ingredients in the drinks we imbibe can help heal the body—it's rare to hear of a mocktail touted just for its flavor and not for how it can improve your mood or support digestion. Zero-proof cocktails coincide with a desire for intentionality—a reflection on overall well-being and wellness.

But you don't need to stop at just the health benefits. Each ingredient also tells a story. When selected with an understanding of that ingredient's background or energy, your mocktail becomes something else entirely. It becomes a potion.

Mysticism, magic, and mocktails go hand-in-hand (and in your hand). They reflect an overall intentionality about life, a desire to live in tune with the universe and one's spirit—to cultivate an existence of health, self-trust and intuition, fulfillment and happiness. Just like someone might perform a cleansing bath ritual for renewal, one can choose nonalcoholic ingredients to nurture that energy within the body.

I can walk you through an example in this very book. In the making of Rose of Remembrance, I selected ingredients for love, spirituality, memory, and healing—a drink to accompany healing from loss. In making and imbibing this recipe, I found myself reminiscing and mourning a wound I didn't even realize was there. When you are aware of not just the healing but the spiritual and folkloric meanings of ingredients—of the energy they hold—your mocktail (and even the process of making it) can become a physical embodiment of spiritual alchemy.

In this book, I will walk you through how your drinks are not just nutritious or delicious but healing—conduits for your magic and mindful healing journey. Through adding each ingredient with meaning and imbibing with intention, your mocktails become infused with something deeper.

So whether you are looking for a drink to tap into the moon's powers of healing and spirituality (like the Moon Goddess Colada with cucumber and coconut milk) or sharing the Rose Quartz Harmon-tea with a guest for open-hearted communication, there's a myriad of ways to craft delicious, elevated nonalcoholic drinks that are as tasty and enchanting as they are magical.

HOW TO USE THIS BOOK

To help you navigate your experience, here is what you will find in this book:

PART 1 GROUNDS MIXOLOGY AND MAGICAL KNOWLEDGE:

For the magically inclined and health-inspired readers, chapter 1 will open your eyes to how drinks have sacred histories and the deeper meaning of what you hold in your cup. Chapter 2 will illuminate how mocktails can be magical and healing and even intertwined into self-care rituals.

For those who are more concerned about mixology, chapter 3 covers the ingredients and tools you will need. It will walk you through the various ways you can get creative in making mocktails and how to substitute for ingredients that don't require nonalcoholic spirits. Chapter 4 covers the process of making a drink—how to shake or muddle, as well as how to turn this process from a labor to a mindful ritual to start the mystical mocktail experience before you even sip.

PART 2 COVERS THE RECIPES, ARRANGED FOR THE VARIOUS PHASES OF YOUR LIFE.

Here, the beverages are divided by intention so that you know where to turn based on where you are in your journey—whether it's "Connection" recipes for gatherings with friends or "Insight" for drinks to accompany intuitive rituals and ceremonies.

"RENEWAL" covers recipes for cleansing, protection, renewal, and new beginnings.

"CONNECTION" covers recipes for love, friendship, gatherings, and the heart.

"WELL-BEING/WELLNESS" covers recipes inspired by holistic health, integrated wellness, and self-care.

"**INSIGHT**" covers recipes for spirituality, psychic insight, clarity, and wisdom to guide you through dark times.

"**MANIFESTATION**" covers recipes for abundance, luck, and attraction, as well as drinks to align and get the vibe right, whether for positivity or prosperity.

Breakout sections are scattered throughout to help you make the most magic out of your drinks. And because you might drink by the season or lunar cycle, the appendixes in the back suggest recipes to pair with those occasions.

In this book, you'll uncover nonalcoholic options for every intention and occasion. There are drinks to heighten your rituals, align with your intentions, or even be a ritual all on their own. From recipes to match or elevate your mood (whether you're doing some self-care or relaxing after a long day), there's a recipe for you.

Along the way, we will discuss the mystical meanings of ingredients and even some health benefits, but please exercise caution. Always use these ingredients mindfully and be aware of how herbal ingredients may counteract with your medicine or medical condition. Consult your doctor if you're unsure. Also, while we will talk about things like manifestation or grieving, nothing replaces doing the work or going to therapy. My hope is, though, that you'll uncover a deeper meaning and magic in your drink recipes and even make your own.

PART 1

Arthurian tales tell of the legendary Holy Grail, a chalice with miraculous healing powers and endless sustenance that could even grant eternal youth. In "The Iliad," Homer describes in detail Nestor's mystical cup, which only he could lift, used to prepare healing drinks for the injured. From wide-mouthed teacups and Viking drinking horns to bowls with inscriptions and elegant stone-carved chalices, these sacred vessels are overflowing with ancient myths and significance. Our glasses and what we contain within them are brimming with potential magic that awaits us.

In part 1, you will unravel the sacred roots of nonalcoholic drinks—many of these ancient spiritual practices persist today. Then we will delve into modern mocktail mixology and how such a drink can be tied to mindful, mystical rituals for healing, self-care, and manifestation. In chapter 3, you will learn the basics of what you need to mix a spellbinding nonalcoholic potion and the unique meaning of your ingredients—even altering a concoction to make it suitable for your palate or how the simple act of squeezing a lemon can become a purifying ritual. This will help prepare the way so that in part 2 you will feel confident in altering recipes to accommodate your preferences and perhaps even making your own mystical mocktails! By connecting to the sacred symbolism of the cup and the ingredients you put in it, you can elevate your nonalcoholic drinks into a magical, mindful beverage for well-being.

CHAPTER 1

MYTHS, MAGIC, AND MIXOLOGY

Potions from the Past to the Present Day

Imbibing meaningful drinks is a rite as old as time. We clink glasses at celebrations, cheers to one's health, have a conversation over hot cocoa, or have a first date at a café. These beverages narrate our lives—they tell stories of nostalgia, bring comfort and warmth, celebrate our cultures and ancestry. They are a form of connection, healing, and nurturance.

Our ancestors saw meaning and myth in everything they drank and ate. It was a form of sustenance and connection with the natural world. Every ingredient had a meaning and story, connected to a cosmic worldview or imbibed in a ritualistic way.

Through looking at these beverages and the rituals that surrounded them, we unravel a deeper meaning and symbolism in what we drink. We can begin to glean how making a drink is an act of alchemy—transforming ingredients to create something new, with story, heart, and meaning—that has the potential to influence how we feel (without the alcohol).

While the focus of ancient drinks often emphasizes alcohol, there are three strong examples (and surely many more) of nonalcoholic sacred drinks that extend deep into the past and, in fact, are still alive today. These findings are limited to research that is available as of this writing, and there will be even more discoveries in the future. To start, we will look at one beverage with which you are probably already familiar: tea.

THE WAY OF TEA

Tea and spirituality go hand-in-hand. Chamomile calms the mind, while chai warms the energy body with spices. Green tea is great for health, the conscious mind, and focus. In today's age, there is a plethora of spiritual, elevating tea mixtures to make this sacred ritual even more potent. While reflecting over a cup of tea is a common trope, there is one tea ritual that sticks out among the others.

The Japanese tea ceremony (called chado or chanoyu) is a ritualized preparation and sharing of tea that has been practiced for hundreds of years. Referred to as "the way of tea," every aspect of this ritual is infused with spiritual meaning, artistry, and intentionality. Sen No Rikyu infused Zen Buddhism into the ceremony to highlight Harmony, Respect, Purity, and Serenity, right down to the hand movements.

At the center of this ceremony is the belief that no meeting or moment could ever fully be repeated, and thus the experience of each moment should be fully treasured. Chanoyu is a practice infused with spirituality and simplicity that thrives to this day in different variations of formality and setting.

The Japanese tea ceremony is an example of how drinks are not just about hydrating the body. They can center our cultural and community experiences, and through integrating intentionality and ceremony into the experience, a cup of tea can become something much, much more than a medicinal beverage—it can become a reflection of our values, our spiritual beliefs, our connection to nature, and the fleeting moment of life at hand. While what we drink can be medicinal and beneficial for the body, it can also connect and bring calm, harmony, and balance to the spirit and the heart.

CACAO CEREMONIES

Touted as a sacred ritual to connect to the plant medicine and magic of the cacao plant, cacao ceremonies are a growing trend in modern alternative spirituality. It is an intentional ritual that highlights connection, gratitude, and reciprocity with ancestors, each other and the earth, resulting in a beverage of both physical and spiritual nourishment.

But drinking cacao for ritual is not a modern invention—the plant has an ancient history dating as far back as 5,300 years ago,[1] and it is one of the most important beverages in Mesoamerican history. It is a drink of cultural heritage and ancestral connection and a divine gift from the gods. As far back as 3,100 years ago, the Olmec buried cacao vessels with sacrificial victims, hinting at a possible belief system where cacao was an integral part of the death and rebirth cycle.[2] These themes are only further echoed through the ancient Maya culture, where cacao (among other fruits) originated from the death of the Maize god.[3] In some versions, the Maize god is buried in "sustenance mountain," from which a tree bearing all fruits sprouts. In others, the deity's severed head is placed on a barren tree that then begins to produce cacao and other fruits. To the ancient Maya people, cacao and other sustenance were part of a divine cosmology and interconnected with sacrifice, death, and regeneration. In some cases, it was a form of generational heritage and reincarnation. In the Popol Vuh, the severed head of the Maize god from the tree spits on and thereby impregnates an underworld maiden. Other Mayan iconography depicts cacao pods as having a human face, and the stone sarcophagus of the Maya king Pakal shows his mother being reborn as a cacao tree.[4] These ancient beliefs paint a picture in which cacao beverages served as part of a greater cosmological worldview—that there was an interconnected nature between drink, sustenance, the earth, ancestors, and the manifestation of deity—how death can give way to new life.

Cacao is a sacred beverage still ingrained in modern Mesoamerican cultures as a form of celebration and connection. Preparing cacao takes great effort and intention—a process many see as a ritual in itself, one infused with love and labor, to share with family and friends and for celebrations.[4] Through crafting it ceremoniously and with intention, one connects to the ancestral lineage of this plant, giving gratitude for its history and medicine.

YERBA MATÉ

Sacred drinks and rituals are all around us—tucked beneath the buzz of the busy modern world. Sometimes, these stories are closer to home than you think. Such was yerba maté for me.

Following the end of WWII, many Polish veterans became expatriates in search of new and safe homes. Argentina opened its arms to immigrants, my grandmother (*babcia*, in Polish) among them. Here, my babcia participated in celebrated Argentinian social customs, among them the sharing of yerba maté. One of these traditional cups and drinking straws caught my eye while I was visiting her, and the story (and preparation) of this traditional drink ensued.

For South America and Argentina, yerba maté is tied to a rich cultural history where the tea is prepared and passed around a social group while conversing. Everyone drinks from the same *bombilla* (a metal straw with a sifter on one end to prevent sipping in the herb). The yerba maté is brewed with care in a dried squash/gourd or wooden cup called a calabash. The leaves are first added and doused with a bit of cold water to prevent burning of the leaves. Hot (but not boiling) water is then poured. The brewer (*cebador*) taste-tests for quality, then the drink is refilled and the cup passed around, everyone sipping and sharing from the same cup.

Yerba maté is not just the drinking of a tea but an act that promotes friendship and bonding. It strengthens community connections and demonstrates unity. In fact, it is not exclusive to Argentina. While yerba maté became a core element of class tensions in Argentina and tied to cultural identity, it originates from the Guarani and Kaingang of Paraguay and Argentina[5] and touts an older heritage back to the ancestors of these Indigenous populations before European colonialism. Ceremonially, yerba maté would be used to facilitate communication with the supernatural for spiritual knowledge or used as a medicine for its energizing properties.[5]

The preparation and drinking of yerba maté enhances bonding and social connections and facilitates authentic conversations. Through the drinking of a communal cup, it is an act of unity that demonstrates the strength of their community and shared cultural identity. It is a gesture of hospitality, and the continuation of these rituals celebrates a rich cultural legacy.

CONNECTION AND CUPS THROUGH TIME

Yerba maté, cacao, and the Japanese tea ceremony are tied to cultural identities and offer an opportunity to bond and connect. It's not just about the taste of the drink or the medicinal value but rather the sum of the experience: the sacred plant, the legacy, and the intentional process of creation are as equal as the health benefits, connection, and sharing.

So while emphasis tends to be placed on alcoholic beverages, nonalcoholic drinks indeed have a rich history of being sacred. These beverages were served to connect to ancestors, celebrate gifts from the gods, or affirm spiritual values. They promote health benefits and continue today as a way to strengthen values, community, and connection through opening the heart. These stories exemplify how our drinks can be a vehicle for something much more—that each ingredient has a story and through the ritual process of creation we can create a spiritual experience for well-being.

CHAPTER 2

MAGIC IN EVERY CUP

Mocktails for Magic, Healing, and Mindfulness

When you imbibe a beverage that is aligned to your intention, you invite that energy into the vessel of your body, and into your life. The glass is symbolic—a chalice of blessings and how you nurture your body and spirit—a potion of potential.

Drinks often accent our lives. We meet in coffee shops with friends or at a bar for a first date. So what can we replace them with? The desire for a healthier lifestyle has been a motivator in the rise of a new type of drink: the modern mocktail.

DEFINING MOCKTAILS

At its most basic level, a mocktail refers to a cocktail without alcohol, but it is often *much* more. Rather than a sugary soda or fancy lemonade, it is an elevated drink with complex flavor profiles and balance, to sip and savor much in the same way someone would a cocktail (but without the alcohol). And now, with nonalcoholic spirits on the rise, there's even more ways to enjoy creative, elevated recipes that are an experience in and of themselves.

Back in the day, these used to be called "virgin drinks." This term had a certain *ick* to it (and I'm personally very glad we moved away from it). But now, we have a plethora of terms to the point where it gets confusing: mocktail, zero-proof cocktail, free-spirited, spirit-free, nonalcoholic—what do all of these mean?

MOCKTAIL—Mocktail is probably by far the most popular term used to refer to nonalcoholic drinks that have the same elevation of a cocktail but without the alcohol—hence the change of the *c* in "cocktail" to an *m*. However, some feel this term lends itself to being inferior in some way—that it is trying to *mock*, or imitate, and it thus insinuates a lesser version. Others assert that it keeps the focus on trying to re-create cocktails (and thus alcohol) rather than nonalcoholic drinks being something different in their own right.

ZERO-PROOF OR ZERO-PROOF COCKTAIL—Others have shifted to terms like zero-proof. In mixology, "proof" is the term used to measure the alcohol content. By US law, proof is twice the percent of alcohol by volume (ABV). For example, if something is 40% ABV, the proof is 80. So, the term "zero-proof" refers to zero alcohol. But this industry-specific language might not be transparent to the average person.

LOW ALCOHOL/LOW ABV—Low alcohol and low ABV refer to drinks that still have alcohol but to a lesser amount. This may be a good choice for those trying to be more mindful about alcohol but not completely abstaining.

NONALCOHOLIC OR NONALCOHOLIC COCKTAIL—Non- or no-alcohol states exactly what it is: no alcohol. It's quite cut and dry, but it still centers the terminology on alcohol, which some may dislike. Some people also use the term "alcohol-free."

COCKTAIL—For some, "cocktail" is synonymous with alcohol (and thus the continued use of it in the terms above can contribute to confusion). However, when you look at phrases such as "a cocktail of factors," or even a shrimp or fruit cocktail, it becomes apparent that the term is not exclusive to alcohol. Rather, it is the mixing of different elements that result in something completely different from its individual parts—and, often, something greater. For me, it emphasizes the magic of alchemy: When you mix different elements together, they can create something entirely unique.

MOCKTAILS AND THE MIND, BODY, AND SPIRIT

Mocktails, zero-proof cocktails, or nonalcoholic drinks—whatever you prefer to call them—are part of a growing desire for a more holistic lifestyle. When we want to be conscious of our health, alcohol may not be the best option. Mocktails offer a more health-conscious way to socially engage and enjoy the experience of a cocktail, without the alcohol or soft drinks.

Increasingly, though, mocktails are part of a bigger trend in mindfulness—being conscious of not only what we are putting into our bodies but how it affects us mentally, emotionally, and spiritually. The mind/body/spirit philosophy emphasizes this intertwined connection. The mind refers to one's mental health—their thoughts and attitudes. The body is the physical: the skin, brain, organs, one's physical experience in the world and their ability to heal and recover. Spirit is about one's sense of hope and connection to all things. It can reflect a belief system or feeling connected and having a sense of purpose. The idea is that these three—often viewed as separate—are in fact intertwined. When stressed, we get headaches, hair might fall out, heart or digestion issues surface. On the opposite side of the spectrum, happiness can boost the immune system, and a walk can positively impact the mind. What we eat, how we feel, what we think, and our senses of meaning are inseparable.

By their very nature, nonalcoholic drinks invite awareness for what we put in our bodies. Compared to soft drinks or super-sweet juices, mocktails are about an elevated drinking experience that you sip and savor, like the intentionality of the Japanese tea ceremony. Compared to alcohol, zero-proof beverages are about how you feel tomorrow or even a week from now—not a momentary high. Take the Sleepy Girl Mocktail, for example. This iconic mixture of tart cherry juice, magnesium, and soda water for peaceful rest took the social media world by storm (for a witchy take on the recipe, check out the Restful Witch in part 2). It exemplified the accessibility of mocktails (with a little innovation) and how nonalcoholic drinks don't have to be just juice and sugar. They can also be a delicious and aesthetically fun way to support the body.

MOCKTAILS, MAGIC, AND RITUALS FOR SELF-CARE

Just like mocktails, modern spirituality has also grown in popularity as a result of a desire for holistic well-being. Mindful rituals can bring healing and a sense of purpose. They emphasize empowerment, intentionality, and well-being. No one bats an eye at the benefits of meditation and mindfulness today. Setting intentions with the moon is commonplace. These mindful rituals for healing and self-care can be integrated into what we drink. Through aligning the herbs, citrus and fruits, vegetables, and essences we mix into our concoctions, we can craft drinks that aren't just about zero alcohol but are potions that transform our physical, mental, emotional, and spiritual well-being.

You can mix cardamom, chamomile, and lavender into a Positivity Potion for celebrating the radiance of the sun during the summer solstice. Vanilla, egg, and orange blossom can combine into a drink to celebrate the renewal of spring (like the Zero-Proof Candlemas Cocktail). You can inspire passion and connection with cinnamon, hibiscus, and pineapple, like in Lunar Passion, or harmony and opening the heart with Rose Quartz Harmon-tea. Through being aware of the energy of different ingredients, as well as their folklore and meaning (and not just their health benefits), you create an elixir.

ENERGY AND INTENTIONALITY

In modern magical and spiritual practices, there is a belief that there is energy in all things. It may be based in animism—a soul in various plants, trees, and the earth—an energetic vibration, or the power of symbols. And it is a principle that has seeped into the mainstream—we send good luck or good vibes, or we might comment on how the energy feels off. Some practice the law of attraction, which asserts that like energy attracts like energy.

When it comes to magical mocktails, the idea is that each ingredient has a different meaning or energy, in addition to its purported health benefits. Oftentimes, there is natural synchronicity between the two. For example, rosemary is associated in magic with purification, peace, clarity, and the mind. Studies have shown that rosemary can be beneficial to cognitive function.[6] When it comes to lavender, we all know it's good for calming the mind.

By adhering to the ancient wisdom and stories of these plants and herbs, we can concoct meaningful, intentional drinks with the awareness of how they will impact our spiritual energy. We can match intentions to the drinks we choose and nurture our bodies with those ingredients to help us attract our desires.

CONNECTION TO THE EARTH

While knowing the meaning of your ingredients matters, so does aligning your life with the changing seasons. Whether you're a witch or not, many spiritual people honor and celebrate the seasonal shifts around them. It might be the benefits of buying food that is in season and how that can impact your health and internal biorhythms. Or it might be making crafts with pine cones or crafting flower crowns.

By putting seasonal ingredients into your mocktails, you not only connect to the magic and benefits of different plants, fruits, and vegetables but also live in tune with nature and the flow of energy and seasons around and within you. By doing so, you can create ease in manifesting the life that you want.

Specifically, many modern witches observe something called the Wheel of the Year. The Wheel of the Year is a modern pagan or witchcraft calendar of holidays—holidays that celebrate the seasonal shifts.

WINTER SOLSTICE **(THE CELEBRATION OF WHICH IS SOMETIMES CALLED YULE)**: The first day of winter and the longest night of the year. From this day forward, the hours of daylight will grow again. It is worshipped as a time for return of the sun, as a metaphor for rebirth, blessings, and transformation.

IMBOLC/CANDLEMAS: A day halfway between winter and spring where the growth of sunlight hours is more apparent. It is a festival to beacon back spring and a day of hope and cleansing.

SPRING EQUINOX **(THE CELEBRATION IS SOMETIMES CALLED OSTARA):** This is the first day of spring and is a day of renewal, new beginnings, fertility, and balance. On this day, there is a temporary balance between the hours of daylight and those of night.

BELTANE: Halfway between spring and summer, this is a sensual day celebrating the fertility of the earth that gives way to abundance. Beauty, romance, flowers, and healing take central stage.

SUMMER SOLSTICE **(THE CELEBRATION OF WHICH IS SOMETIMES CALLED LITHA)**: The first day of summer and the day with the longest hours of daylight. With the sun in full force, it is often a time of power and manifestation but also warmth, positivity, and connection.

LAMMAS/LUGHNASADH: Halfway between summer and fall, this day also celebrates the first harvest. It is a day of gratitude and breaking bread (and oftentimes baking it too!).

AUTUMN EQUINOX **(THE CELEBRATION OF WHICH IS SOMETIMES CALLED MABON):** This day is not just about the first day of fall but also balance. While the autumn equinox witnesses a momentary balance between hours of daylight and hours of dark, it is a reminder that the hours of daylight will soon wane. It's also the second harvest of harvest season.

SAMHAIN: Halfway between fall and winter, it is the final harvest celebration and a day of the dead. It often coincides with Halloween celebrations, a time where the "veil" between worlds feels thin and people honor ancestors and those who have passed.

Your experience of the seasons may vary based on where you are in the world. But honoring these seasonal shifts provides reflection on life themes—they offer a time to focus on certain areas of your life for healing, growth, and magic.

THE MOON

You've probably heard of setting intentions with the moon or releasing, cleansing, and purifying. You might pull tarot cards for insight, charge moon water, light candles for manifestation, or take a moon bath. It stems from a belief that the moon has certain spiritual energy and that each moon phase or entire lunar cycle has a distinct energy that can be fruitful for spiritual purposes. These rituals often highlight themes of mindfulness, healing, and empowerment.

Through aligning with the moon, many witches find opportunities for healing—they reflect on life, as the full moon illuminates their innermost feelings and emphasizes intuition. It bolsters their spells and rituals to live in greater alignment with the universe. In this way, mindfulness means being conscious of the moon's cycles and their effects on us or even just using them to gauge how life is unfolding. Also, a moon ritual can be empowering—it takes one's healing journey into their own hands and arms spiritual people with the means to bring greater peace and awareness into their life, rather than be at the whims of others. It's about becoming in alignment with the life one wants to lead.

MOON AND WATER

The moon is often associated with water because of its apparent gravitational impact over the seas. The moon creates the high and low tides that dictate ocean life. Shellfish close and open based on the phase of the moon and its resulting currents; baby turtles use the moon to find the shore. Many magical folks recognize this connection and create moon water—charging water with the energy of the full moon—which can be added to baths, rituals, and more. So from that angle, a liquid libation is a perfect way to connect with the moon.

MOON AND EARTH

The moon is vital not just to water but to the earth. The moon was once much closer to earth and very likely had an impact on the evolution of life on earth. Many farmers and gardeners observe this connection with lunar gardening—the belief that certain phases of the moon (or even seasonal moons) are beneficial for different types of plants and plant care, such as when to plant, harvest, or prune.

There are seasonal moons, now commonly known as monthly moons because of our Gregorian calendar, like the flower moon or blood moon. Those lunar names highlight a seasonal energy that is prominent under that lunation. In fact, the end of summer into fall is harvest season, whereby the moon plays an important role in the harvesting of plants.

Between these two, the moon has a very real connection in nurturing the food we eat and the ingredients we put into our drinks. So it's through not just the moon's connection to water but also its connection to these ingredients that mocktails can very much become lunar libations and a vessel for your lunar self-care and mindful moon rituals.

Your mocktails can be perfect for celebrating the moon: You can include ingredients aligned to your lunar intention, match your moon ritual to a potion with corresponding edible ingredients, or even just make a potion for the moon as a ritual in itself. For this very purpose, I've included an appendix on corresponding lunar drinks in the book.

CHAPTER 3

WHAT YOU NEED TO MAKE a MAGICAL MOCKTAIL

I still remember the first time I received an order for a mocktail. A virgin mojito had just popped out of the receipt printer at my first bartending job at California Pizza Kitchen. Working with just soda water, lime, sugary syrups, and mint, I couldn't create something that lived up to the original cocktail. There weren't the nonalcoholic spirits that there are today or the creativity around them. The mixology world has certainly come a long way since then.

The desire for elevated recipes has led to the incorporation of mixology techniques that integrate the benefits and flavors of herbs, and even vinegar. Through modern mixology, you can incorporate health-conscious ingredients in many ways. Now, with spirit-free alternatives, there are even more ways to enjoy creative, elevated drinks that are an experience in and of themselves.

MOCKTAIL BASES

NONALCOHOLIC SPIRITS

Thanks to the mocktail and zero-proof movement, there is innovation in the market that could change mocktails forever: zero-proof spirits. Your virgin beverages no longer need to be just juices or sparkling sodas. By law, as long as they do not contain more than 0.5% alcohol by volume (ABV),[7] they can be advertised as nonalcoholic (this pertains to nonalcoholic wine and beer too). Given that these are new to the market, many people aren't quite sure what they are or what to make of them (yet).

HOW ARE NONALCOHOLIC SPIRITS MADE?

Nonalcoholic spirits are made in a variety of different ways: using glycerin to infuse flavors; stopping alcohol from forming during the fermentation process; distilling and removing alcohol afterward; infusing water, botanicals, essences, and hydrosols. Some of these (such as infusing glycerin) are things you can even try at home.

Unlike alcohol, there isn't a lot of guidance on how it's created—each brand creates their version using what works best for them, to try to replicate the flavor notes of the most popular alcohol spirits or even to create something entirely different. And for this reason, each nonalcoholic spirit (even spirit-specific substitutions, such as tequila replacements) has an entirely different flavor profile.

THE CONCERNS AND BENEFITS OF NONALCOHOLIC SPIRITS

As a new industry, there's a lot of uncharted territory that can be hard to navigate. For one, there is such a variance between brands that you might dislike one brand's nonalcoholic tequila replacement but love another's. Sometimes, a nonalcoholic spirit will be amazing enough to enjoy straight. Other times, it delivers only when in a mixed drink. That means that you may have to try a few different nonalcoholic spirit brands before really finding the ones you like.

While there can be a downside to nonalcoholic spirits, the truth is they answer a call in the industry. Previously, crafting mocktails required relying on fruits, juices, and soda water. Nonalcoholic spirits offer an exciting possibility where you can enjoy that "adult," elevated cocktail-like experience where you can sip and savor the artistry, without the alcohol. Oftentimes, you can infuse these nonalcoholic spirits in the same way you might infuse alcohol (albeit longer), allowing for the effortless integration of unique flavors.

WHERE TO BUY NONALCOHOLIC SPIRITS?

More and more nonalcoholic spirits are popping up in grocery stores, markets, and wine/alcohol specialty stores. They are often tucked into the alcohol aisle, so it may take some time searching to find it (especially if it's nonalcoholic wine, as the bottles look quite the same). And because they are nonalcoholic, you can often easily order them online for delivery, which makes it much easier to find the replacement you're looking for.

NONALCOHOLIC BEERS, WINE, AND BITTERS

Compared to traditional spirits, beverages like wine and beer have much less alcohol content. And as a result, there are a lot of great nonalcoholic options for these that have been around for a while. This is great for magical mocktail making or even having an option to drink straight when going alcohol free.

NONALCOHOLIC BEER: While beer typically ranges anywhere from 2% to 15% alcohol, nonalcoholic beers can have as little as zero alcohol content. They are produced much in the same way as beer—with water, hops, yeast, and grains.

Nonalcoholic beers have four ways of handling the no-alcohol part: *dealcoholizing,* where the alcohol is removed after; *controlled fermentation,* where the fermentation process is stopped before it produces alcohol; *dilution,* where water is added to reduce the alcohol by volume; and *simulated fermentation,* where the fermentation process is skipped entirely but ingredients are added to simulate it.

NONALCOHOLIC WINE: Today, alcohol-free wines are increasing in popularity. You can find dealcoholized versions of red, white, and even sparkling wines. The most common terms used are "nonalcoholic," "dealcoholized," and "alcohol removed." While traditionally wine can be anywhere from 5.5% to 25% alcohol, dealcoholized and alcohol-removed wine is wine that has been fully fermented but had most or all of its alcohol removed to below the legal 0.5% limit. Many of these start out as traditional wine, where the alcohol is thereby removed in one of three ways: reverse osmosis, vacuum distillation, or spinning cone columns. Through these industrial processes, the alcohol content can be brought to legal level—and often less than what you'd find in fermented drinks like kombucha. After the removal, blending may occur to re-create some of the mouthfeel and flavors removed by these processes.

BITTERS: Many bitters (like Angostura) have origins as herbal remedies and are essential in many of today's favorite cocktails. But these highly concentrated flavors are traditionally made using alcohol to infuse botanicals—they can have 35%–45% ABV.

This is where it gets into gray territory. Because you're using only a few drops at a time, it can often be diluted to less than the 0.5% limit when added to a mocktail. So some people are okay incorporating alcoholic bitters into their nonalcoholic drinks.

However, there are nonalcoholic alternatives for those who prefer to avoid them. All The Bitter has great sans-alcohol bitters (like lavender, orange, and aromatic, re-creating some of the classics) that can be used in both traditional and alcohol-free cocktails.

TEAS, HERBAL INFUSIONS, AND DECOCTIONS

Tea and herbal infusions are some of my favorite ways to replace alcohol in mocktails. For one, they have tannins—those naturally occurring polyphenols that give bitter flavors often found in alcohols like wine and barrel-aged spirits. These astringent flavors are often a core part of mixology (hence "*bitters*"). Not only can teas be a way to add these bitter qualities to recipes but also they can add numerous health benefits *and* help make up for the volume lost in cocktails made without alcohol. This way, your mocktails don't have to be limited to flavored lemonades or limeades or soda waters, or rely on specialty syrups for unique flavors. However, tea in a mocktail can quickly become watery since it is water-based and thus may require specific preparations like using two tea bags or freezing it into cubes you can then add to your mocktail (as you'll see in part 2). Teas may not be an equal replacement for alcohol but create something truly unique and different, and perhaps even better. And compared to nonalcoholic spirits, they are pretty much accessible around the world and can be made within minutes.

TYPES OF TEAS

Tea refers to drinks produced from steeping the leaves and buds of the *Camellia sinensis* plant. But having been cultivated since at least since 1122 BCE (and possibly as far back as 2737 BCE according to its founding myth),[8] there are many different types of teas that have extremely different flavor profiles and applications for your magical mocktails:

- WHITE TEA is made from the youngest leaves and buds of the *C. sinensis* plant. These are often the most tender parts and undergo minimal processing, leading to a gentle, more delicate, or even floral expression. Just like black or green tea, there can be different types or blends, such as pomegranate white tea.
- In GREEN TEA, the leaves of the *C. sinensis* plant are steamed or pan-fried after harvesting to prevent the oxidation process. Per the name, it has a distinct green color and often grassy flavor.
- There are different types, too, like JASMINE GREEN TEA, in which the leaves are infused with the fragrant aroma of jasmine blossoms. This tea is often more subtle and floral.
- MATCHA is a type of green tea but unique in its cultivation, flavor, and mouthfeel. The leaves are ground into a fine powder, and the plants intended for matcha are often grown in the shade, causing chemical changes in the plant. It is also the staple tea in the Japanese tea ceremony mentioned in chapter 1.

- In BLACK TEA, the leaves of the *C. sinensis* plant undergo oxidation. They have a rich, dark color and a more astringent, bitter, and robust flavor. There are many popular variations or blends of this, such as:
- EARL GREY, where black tea is blended with oil from the bergamot orange.
- CHAI TEA (also known as masala chai), originating from India, where it is spiced with cardamom, cinnamon, ginger, clove, and more.
- OOLONG TEA falls in the middle of black and green tea. It undergoes a shorter oxidation and can have a wide range of flavors, expression, and aromas between the two.

HERBAL "TEAS," INFUSIONS, AND DECOCTIONS

In popular culture, "tea" is commonly used to refer to any beverage where herbal ingredients are steeped in hot water, such as hibiscus or chamomile. Technically, those aren't really "tea" but herbal infusions/tisanes (created by steeping) or decoctions (created by boiling).

- Common HERBAL TEAS include hibiscus, chamomile, or even lavender. These really carry the flavor profile of the ingredient—and also the part of the plant that is used.
- YERBA MATÉ (as you might recall from chapter 1) has its own cultural heritage. It is made from *Ilex paraguariensis,* a plant species of holly native to South America.

There are more herbal teas and infusions out there—as many as there are edible, medicinal plant species in the world. Allow your curiosity to lead you to such beverages and how they can be integrated into your mystical mocktails.

CITRUS MAGIC AND MOCKTAILS

From aromatizing soaps to lemon meringue, citrus has an unmatched ability to uplift energy. Many varieties tout health benefits and are packed with antioxidants like vitamin C. But citrus also plays a crucial role in your mystical mocktails as well—it adds acidity to balance infusions and syrups and brighten recipes with its oils. And many of them have a deeper symbolism and magic.

Below you'll find the mystical meaning of the most common citrus used in mixology. When you are aware of their energy, you can transform the simple act of squeezing juice into your drink into a mood-boosting and cleansing ritual, or elevate a basic lemonade into one with aligned luscious herbs and spices to boost your energy. Just remember: When it comes to citrus, fresh is always best. Prejuiced citrus from

the grocery store often has additives to become shelf stable, and that can change the balance of your drinks. But always use what is accessible and easiest for you.

LEMON: Lemon is a fast favorite for many. It has a refreshing, zesty quality that can bring inspiration and joy to a space and inspire positive connection. This bright, awakening citrus is popular in cleansing scents and soaps, so it should be of little surprise that lemon is also a common ingredient for cleansing and purification in rituals. In fact, lemon's association with the moon (which just so happens to also be lemon-shaped) makes it a perfect ingredient for lunar mocktails, especially for uplifting and renewal.

LIME: Next to lemon, lime is one of the most popular citruses used to balance drink recipes. But unlike lemon, lime is associated with the sun, and its magical properties lean toward removing hexes and dispelling ill will. In breaking energetic blockages, lime can also make way for healing and love.

ORANGE: While it may not be as acidic as lemon or lime, orange plays a central role in many drink recipes, from its awakening juice to cordials used for classics like the sidecar or Cadillac margarita. Mixology's love of orange even extends to its blossoms: You can add orange blossom (or flower) water (available online at sites like Amazon or in mixology specialty stores) to homemade grenadine or add it as an aromatic spritz atop a mocktail. Orange is also associated with the sun and used in magic to bring joy, good health, and even inspiration. In many Eastern traditions, varieties of this fruit are given as gifts for happiness and prosperity at the New Year. As a blossom, orange can inspire beauty and bless unions.

GRAPEFRUIT: Grapefruit's gentle tanginess can be just the touch a drink needs for light acidity and relaxation. It has become iconic in revitalizing recipes like the greyhound or paloma and can even be beneficial for the skin and beauty. In Western magical practices, it is associated with purification and positivity and may help improve one's mood.

CONSCIOUS MAGIC: REDUCING WASTE

When using citrus for drinks, we're often left with the peel and discarded pith and pulp. In being intentional about ingredients, you can also use them mindfully. Through finding innovative ways to extend their use, you can not only cut down on waste but also accessorize your mystical recipes with corresponding rituals. Here are some ways these peels can be cross-used to reduce waste and integrate the magic of citrus in other areas:

- Infuse leftover peels into a syrup.
- Place citrus discards in simmer pots to aromatize the air.
- Dry the peels and incorporate them into potpourri blends.
- Blend dried peels into a powder for other food or as magical candle dressings.
- Soak citrus discards in vinegar for a homemade cleaner.
- Candy the peels and even dip them in chocolate.
- Make citrus marmalades from peels to uplift your day.
- Carve a word or sacred symbol into leftover peels for a magical sigil.
- Pour candle wax and wicks into leftover citrus halves for cleansing and uplifting ritual candles.

SWEETENERS

While I will cover cane sugar and simple syrup below, many recipes in this book lean on natural sweeteners, like maple syrup, honey, and agave. Classic simple syrup still very much has a place in mocktail mixology, but it's about being intentional in how we use it. Now, let's get into the various sweeteners you can use for your mocktails and their mystical properties!

SUGAR

The sweetener that most of us are familiar with is white, refined, and overprocessed table sugar. It is also tied to a long and dark history of colonialism and slavery. While table sugar is widely available (and arguably overused) today, it was once a rarer commodity. In magic, it is used in attraction spells for love and lust or to "sweeten" someone up to you (to win their favor). But there are also other types of less refined sugar that can be used in mixology:

DEMERARA: A light brown sugar with large granules that is minimally processed, thus naturally maintaining low amounts of molasses for a richer flavor.

BROWN SUGAR: Often made by adding molasses back in after refinement, usually having smaller grains.

SIMPLE SYRUP: Sugar is often incorporated into mixology through simple syrup, made of equal parts sugar and hot water. Because of the flavor profile, it is easy to infuse additional flavors into simple syrup by steeping or boiling herbs, like a tea.

HONEY: A natural sweetener, honey was among the first sweeteners known to the world and as such was seen as divine. It was used for offerings and spiritual purposes. The result of hardworking bees, it is associated with harvest, community, and goddess worship. It is also a common ingredient in spells for "sweetening" someone up to you, such as honey jars.

HONEY SYRUP: In mixology, honey is mixed with equal or less parts hot water to allow for easier integration into drinks. Through the addition of warm water, you can also infuse an herbal remedy, such as the Rose-Honey Syrup I use in some recipes in part 2. However, the flavor of honey is quite pronounced, and it can be hard for more subtle flavors to come through.

MAPLE: Maple syrup is another natural sweetener alternative and one you can add directly to drinks, although its benefits can depend a lot on its cultivation and processing. For that reason, maple syrup can vary from brand to brand, so be sure to start with less and add more to taste. In magical folklore, its energy can benefit intentions of longevity, money, and love. I also love to use it for anything "tree" related, such as forest energy, remaining grounded, or connecting to one's roots for ancestral wisdom.

In drinks, I find that maple adds a woodsy, subtly sweet, and earthy flavor, with notes of caramel and vanilla. A little goes a long way, and it can be a dynamic and flavorful addition to your magical mocktails.

AGAVE: The rich cultural history of this sacred plant has given way to pulque through fermentation and tequila and mezcal when distilled.

But its nectar is also used as a natural and beneficial sweetener! In magic, it is associated with lust and love, and with its unique life cycle it is a favorite of mine to include in mocktails for revival. It is also a great way to re-create some of those tequila and mezcal essences, without the alcohol. With its viscosity, you can add agave directly to your drink recipes, but you can also mix it with an equal amount of an herbal infusion, as I do with lavender in the Magical Margarita(s) in part 2, chapter 5.

GRENADINE: Grenadine is the syrup responsible for the iconic Shirley Temple and tequila sunrise, giving a burgundy-red layered effect. However, the grenadine you buy from the store is often sugary and overprocessed. You can easily make it at home, where you can control what goes in it and make something more magical.

Grenadine is traditionally made from pomegranate juice, with a minor citrus element such as orange blossom water or a small amount of lemon juice. Pomegranate is associated with abundance, fertility, and creativity in witchcraft as well as the Greek goddess of the underworld, Persephone.

For homemade grenadine, I like to use 1 cup pomegranate to ¼ cup sweetener.

OTHER MOCKTAIL MIXOLOGY INGREDIENTS

ORANGE BLOSSOM/FLOWER WATER: A nonalcoholic fragrant water (hydrosol) of orange blossoms, produced as the by-product of distilling the flowers of the bitter orange tree. This aromatic water invokes the alluring vibrancy of orange blossoms with each sip and makes the most enchanting recipes. It can be purchased online, or from specialty or Middle Eastern stores.

TONIC WATER: Compared to soda water, tonic water is more bitter. It is made with quinine from the cinchona tree.

SODA WATER: Carbonated water is created by infusing water with carbon dioxide gas, sometimes with added minerals. Along with tonic water, it helps to add more volume to your drink recipes and add a fizzy quality.

ROSE WATER: Just like orange blossom water, rose water is also a nonalcoholic hydrosol, made from distilling rose petals. It is a beautiful ingredient to add for the loving energy of rose. Just be sure to use food-grade, mixology-specific rose water, as rose water for beauty products can have other added ingredients.

VINEGAR: This sour and acidic ingredient has grown in popularity for its purported health benefits, like aiding digestion. Made from the fermentation of alcohol whereby bacteria converts ethanol into acetic acid, vinegar can add body and dynamic flavor to many mocktails. You can even make your own shrubs or drinking vinegars!

EXTRACTS: Often used in baking, extracts are concentrated flavorings made by soaking these ingredients, such as vanilla or peppermint, in a solution of both alcohol and water. These can be another way to integrate unique flavors. Like bitters, though, they have an alcohol content of around 35%, so it's important to be mindful of their use if you're going to incorporate them.

ADJUSTING YOUR RECIPES

While mocktail mixology rides on the back of the craft cocktail movement, you gain a certain freedom when you remove alcohol from the balance of your cocktails. Get innovative in how you incorporate the flavor you want—make the recipes work for you and your flavor preferences.

Don't want to use nonalcoholic orange bitters? Try muddling an orange peel for fresh orange oil. Prefer your recipe on the sour side or sweeter? Rebalance the ratio by adding more citrus or more sweetener (just remember you can always add more, but you can't take it out).

Our flavor preferences are as unique as our magic in this world. Don't be afraid to experiment and adjust things to make them work for you.

TOOLS

Before you're ready to whip up some mystical mocktails, you'll need to make sure you have the right tools. Just like the tools on your altar help cast spells, each bartending tool serves a purpose. While I'll offer budget suggestions and alternatives, having the right tools can help you easily and efficiently whip up potions in no time.

THE SHAKER: The iconic symbol of mixology. The shaker helps to aerate, chill, and balance as you mix your drinks with ice. There are two shakers most used today:

- **The Boston Shaker:** Consists of two "cones," one smaller and one larger, that interlock inside each other. Some are dual metal tins, and other times one will be metal and the other glass.
- **The Cobbler Shaker:** This shaker consists of a larger metal or glass tin and a top with a strainer built in. It combines a strainer and shaker in one, eliminating the need for purchasing a separate strainer. However, these are not as versatile and are often more susceptible to getting stuck.

JIGGER: In mixology, the jigger is a typical measuring tool. Oftentimes, it consists of a cone on either side, where one measures 1 ounce and the other 1½–2 ounces. Markers on the side indicate finer increments like ½ or ¼ ounce. Measuring is essential to crafting a mocktail that is as delicious as it is magical. In a pinch, you can convert ounces to tablespoons and use a tablespoon measurer: 1 tablespoon is equal to ½ ounce.

STRAINERS: Health- and energy-conscious recipes often call for fresh ingredients, herbs, and spices. Strainers help separate debris from your finished elixir.

- **Hawthorne Strainer:** A strainer with coils and larger holes that perfectly clasps the edge of your Boston shaker. If using a cobbler shaker, then you may not need this.
- **Fine-Mesh or Tea Strainer:** With tiny or "fine" holes, this strainer catches smaller debris such as ground spices and ice shards. It is often used in conjunction with the Hawthorne strainer, called "double straining."

MUDDLER: Muddlers help to break down fresh ingredients, like cucumber or cherry. They can be used to express oils from herbs, such as mint. In a pinch you can use a wooden spoon.

CITRUS JUICER: When it comes to fresh citrus, having a handheld citrus squeezer makes all the difference!

Having the right tools will help make mixing mocktails easier for you. But they don't need to be mundane. Each tool offers the opportunity for intentionality and magic. In the next part we will talk about how to make using them a ritual in itself.

CHAPTER 4

MIXING MOCKTAIL MAGIC

The Ritual Of Mindful Mocktails

Through integrating a mindfulness practice into your beverage experience, you can make any sip a ritual infused with intention and magic. Mindfulness is the act of being fully engaged in the present moment—not tomorrow, yesterday, or what you need to do tonight—and is a great way to bring harmony between body, spirit, and mind. Luckily, mixing a drink offers plenty of opportunities to bring your awareness to the moment, before savoring the flavor and benefits of your magical mocktail. Doing so can really help you connect to the magic of your glass (regardless of what's in it) and be more present as you unwind and enjoy the magic of your recipes. In the previous section, you learned about the various ingredients of a drink and what tools you might use in making one. Here's how you can infuse them with a mindfulness practice, how to use the tools, and make your mocktail magical with ease.

SETTING THE STAGE

BREATH: Breathing is a great way to both clear your mind and bring it to the present—and a perfect way to initiate your mocktail-making ritual! Begin with a few deep, intentional breaths, breathing slowly into your belly and bringing your focus to the sound and sensation of inhaling and exhaling. Breathe out the thoughts and happenings of the day and bring your senses to the present moment. As you begin to mix your mocktail, match the flow of your breath to the rhythm of mixing, shaking, or muddling. And when you enjoy the final creation, align your breath with each sip: inhale, sip, and swallow, then exhale. While this may prolong the creation of your libation, it will also make it more intentional and relaxing, bringing your mind to the energy of each ingredient, to truly savor the fruits of your effort and the energy and benefits of your drink.

INTENTION: Making an intentional mocktail means being aware of what you are imbibing. As you saw in the previous chapter, each ingredient has a role to play—both magically and mundanely. As you add each ingredient, do so with intention. Focus on what that ingredient adds (in both spiritual energy and health benefits) to your concoction or simply why you are adding it to the drink—such as citrus to cleanse or even just balance the sweetness of the drink. You can reference the herbology appendix to learn more about the energy of each ingredient.

THE SENSES: Mixology has endless opportunities to utilize your senses and bring your mind to now. Adding a fresh or dried herbal ingredient, like rosemary? Allow yourself to enjoy its aroma and the texture of the herb before dropping it into your mixing tin. Making a shaken or stirred drink? As you shake or stir, notice the gradual change in temperature. Tuning in to your senses as you mix will help you savor the recipe you are creating, feel gratitude for the earth's abundance, and also invite your awareness to be present in the intention of the moment.

WAYS OF MIXING

MUDDLING: Muddling mashes herbs or fruit to better infuse their flavors into drinks and is another great way to integrate intention, magic, and mindfulness into a drink. Using an official muddler or even a big wooden spoon, you firmly stamp down on a fresh ingredient and then slightly turn to help break that ingredient apart. Focus on the pressing down and twisting movement as you muddle—you can visualize muddling away the energy of the day, blockages, or any unwanted thoughts.

SHAKE-IT-OFF: Shaking aerates, chills, and dilutes drinks to give them better balance, texture, and integrated flavor. And in magic, you can think of it as your cauldron where your potions alchemically mix, infused with intention—or like a drum or rattle with which you summon up energy for your intention. Perhaps you're having a hard time clearing your mind or releasing the energy of the day. Make a drink that involves a shaker and use the movement to visualize shaking off (or out) the energy! You can also use shaking to integrate movement and sound to raise energy toward your intention (and infuse it into your potion). To shake, place all your ingredients in your shaker, then add one large scoop of ice. Close your shaker and shake for about 8–15 seconds (shorter for a mocktail being served over ice, longer for one being served chilled but without ice). When it comes to mocktails that use teas, you may not need to shake as long; otherwise, your recipe may be too watery. Over time, you will develop a sense for the perfect duration, dependent on your own taste and technique.

STRAINING AND DOUBLE STRAINING: After your drink is shaken, you can use a strainer to separate large chunks of fresh ingredients or fine ice shards and spices from your finished potion. Double straining uses both the Hawthorne strainer and fine-mesh strainer: Place the Hawthorne strainer on the mixing tin and pour the liquid through a fine-mesh strainer over the beverage glass. A tight strain refers to pushing the metal plate of your Hawthorne strainer to the very lip of the tin as you pour, so that it covers the coils and less debris comes out. While this straining may seem mundane, you can envision it as a metaphorical sifter: creating a smooth, alchemical mixture while leaving unwanted energetic "debris" or details behind.

STIRRING YOUR BREW: Stirring is one way to gently combine and chill ingredients in mixology. This traditionally involves a mixing glass and ice, but in mocktails it is more so stirring a built drink in your glass. Stirring a drink (versus shaking it) still chills the recipe but adds less aeration. Plus, it's a little more peaceful and intentional! Listen to the sound of the clinking as you stir and feel the gradual temperature change in your drink—perhaps even watching the ingredients gently mix like a magical brew. You can also add some magical ritual to your creation depending on the direction you stir. Stir clockwise to invoke—envisioning what you are manifesting or bringing into being, whether a peaceful moment, self-care, or abundance. Stir counterclockwise to cleanse and release.

FINISHING TOUCHES

FRESH AND AROMATIC GARNISHES: The presentation of your mystical mocktail deserves just as much attention as the drink-making process. The garnish you add to your recipe can be a potent aromatic not just to set the mood with aesthetic appeal but to enchant the senses. You can use fresh garnishes (such as rosemary, mint, or lavender) for the power of their scent to clear the mind or to bring a sense of peace or an orange peel to add uplifting citrus aromas. You can even use an edible flower to work with the attracting essence or magic of flowers. Garnishes may seem minute, but they greet your nose before each sip. The power of their aroma can set the tone for each sip you take, help elevate your drinking experience, and inspire conscious thinking. Learn more about the magical potential of your garnishes in chapter 7.

EXPRESSING A PEEL: Expressing a peel is a common mixology garnish that adds fresh citrus oils into a recipe. To do so, you peel a piece of citrus and hold it above the glass, rind facing the drink. Squeeze the sides of the peel and the oils should "express," or shoot out, over the drink. Then wipe the rind along the rim of the glass. Twist the peel and balance it on the edge of the glass—there's nothing quite as uplifting as citrus oil with each sip.

ENJOYING YOUR MYSTICAL MOCKTAIL

And after all that hard work, allow yourself to truly appreciate the creation of your conscious elixir! Enjoy the sensation of the visual appeal—the color of the drink—and the smell before you even take your first sip. As you sip, notice the texture of the drink and the layers of flavor. And as you swallow, pay attention to how it goes down your throat and even how it impacts how you feel—your energy, mood, and thoughts. And most importantly (since we're talking about magical mocktails), reflect on what you are bringing into your life with each sip—nourishing your body and energy with that intention through a vibrant potion. Being intentional about enjoying your drink makes each concoction more savory and memorable and helps you tune in to the magic of the recipe.

PART 2: RECIPES

Cups are a vessel. They hold sustenance that nourishes both spirit and body but can also be a symbol of blessings we allow to flow into our life. And now, you can invite magic and mindfulness with each sip of a mystical mocktail. Luxuriate your body in a rose and calendula tea bath while sipping on the Flower Moon Mocktail to invite beauty, peace, and healing under the luminescent May full moon. Invoke new beginnings and renewal while reflecting on the fleeting nature of life with the pink Cherry Blossom Beverage or cultivate inner peace in the present moment with the cucumber and rosemary Jasmine Peace Potion. What you put in your glass has the potential to elevate how you feel, transform your mindset and day, and cultivate a life of alignment and well-being.

In the following pages you will unlock 60 nonalcoholic recipes to fill your cup, whether sipping a drink to accompany your moon ritual, invite connection with a friend, or manifest blessings and call in a prosperous New Year. Organized by intention, you'll find potions for new beginnings and cleansing in "Renewal," such as the Clearing Cucumber and Coconut Gimlet to unwind after a long day. Inspire authentic, heart-to-heart connections to restore your cup with the nonalcoholic cocktails in chapter 6 or focus on self-care and well-being with drinks like the apple and kombucha Winter Wellness in chapter 7. In "Insight," recipes for those moments where you need spiritual insight await you. And, finally, in "Manifestation," you'll find beverages to bring good vibes and blessings, like the spiced mandarin Blessing Mimosa Bombs for an enchanting nonalcoholic mimosa. Along the way, breakout sections will help take your magic beyond the glass, from crafting cleansing smoke bundles from leftover herbs to clear energy or casting sweetening spells that match the ingredients in your mocktail to manifest.

To help open your mind to the magic of your glass, hidden gems await you in each recipe. In addition to core themes, each zero-proof cocktail has optional "Affirmations to Sip By" that you can recite with the drink to infuse mindfulness into the recipe or even to inspire your own affirmations.

Every potion is matched with a brief "Beyond the Glass" reflection or exploration of an ingredient, technique, crystal, or ritual to help you elevate your mindfulness. And to help you adapt recipes, you'll find optional substitutions and additions as well. In case you're not using nonalcoholic spirits, you may decide to double the recipe. Preparations, such as white tea or syrups, can be found in the appendix at the back of the book.

AFFIRMATIONS TO SIP BY:

With each sip, I relax and release.

My mind is refreshed, and my energy is clear.

I foster inner peace and renewal.

Don't be afraid to experiment and make the recipes your own too. Mocktails can coincide with the stories or phases of your life, and as you work through part 2, you may want to express your own experiences through customized, magical, alchemical elixirs.

CHAPTER 5

RENEWAL

Recipes for Purification, Protection, and New Beginnings

Every journey begins with a fresh start. Like the new moon's absence from the sky, we might not be able to see the road forward, but it's soon to come nonetheless. Whether you are renewing your energy, purifying patterns from the past, or setting firm boundaries to begin anew, these potions will fill your cup along the way. After all, there's nothing quite like a drink to refresh mind, body, and spirit.

Sip the renewing power of the new moon with the Clearing Cucumber and Coconut Gimlet or relight your inner hope with the Zero-Proof Candlemas Cocktail. Clear blockages to success and open doors with the Mango and Mandarin Road-Opening Mocktail. Through learning about the energetic potential of salt in mixology and magic and how to reuse herbs to craft cleansing herbal bundles, you will take ownership of your energy to have the new beginning you deserve.

And because an equally important part of new beginnings is clearing blockages and setting boundaries, this section will also have recipes for purification and protection, such as Cosmo-cally Protected with cranberry and blueberry or the Purifying Paloma with jalapeño. Whether starting on a new path or just looking for a rejuvenating sip, these potions, herbs, and rituals will clear bad vibes and restore your spirit.

AFFIRMATIONS TO SIP BY:

With each sip, I release and relax.

My mind is refreshed and clear.

I choose inner peace and new beginnings.

CLEARING CUCUMBER AND COCONUT GIMLET

Rejuvenation, Calm, New Beginnings

Relax and refresh your energy with this simple cucumber, mint, and coconut no-alcohol gimlet. Mint and cucumber refresh and uplift the mind in this zesty concoction, while lime and coconut clear and soothe your senses. With a choice of simple syrup, this is the perfect sip to dispel negative energy and rejuvenate. Imbibe when you need some rest and renewal—it's hard to go wrong with a cucumber gimlet.

SERVES 1

4 mint leaves for refreshing the mind

2 thin slices cucumber

¾ ounce Lemongrass Simple Syrup or classic Simple Syrup (page 199 in the appendix) for clearing energy

1 ounce freshly squeezed lime juice

1½ ounces coconut water for inner purification

Cucumber peel and mint sprig, for garnish

1 In your shaker, place the mint and cucumber to refresh and rejuvenate. Add the lemongrass syrup and muddle the cucumber and mint so that their flavors better integrate into the recipe.

2 Add the lime juice, using the hex-breaking energy of the citrus and the kinetic motion of having squeezed the fruit to "squeeze" out any frustrations or blockages.

3 Add the coconut water for spirituality and purification. Add ice and shake.

4 Strain into a martini glass or coupe and garnish to add a renewing scent of mint with each sip.

BEYOND THE GLASS

The new moon (when the moon is absent from the sky, positioned between the Earth and the sun) is a symbolic time of renewal. While the waxing crescent will soon show in the sky, its momentary absence is a reminder of how we all need renewal before being able to start fresh or begin something new. With coconut water and cucumber, this drink is also attuned to the energy of the new moon. Like the moon, allow yourself time to refresh without expectations and know that your energy (and inner light) will naturally replenish with rest.

AFFIRMATIONS TO SIP BY:
Like a flower blossoming, I turn a new leaf.
Limitless positivity is renewed deep within me.
I am filled with love and a new sense of appreciation.

CHERRY BLOSSOM BEVERAGE

Renewal, Beauty, Love

Invoke renewal and capture the beauty of the moment with this sakura (cherry) blossom, grapefruit, and rose elixir. Inspired by sakura blossom season in Japan, this floral recipe is a celebration of rebirth, youth, beauty, and the fleeting nature of life. Sakura blossom brings such energy here through its powdered form, also used in baking and other goods, and it can be found online or in Asian markets. Refreshing grapefruit cleanses and uplifts your taste buds (and energy), while rose tea inspires love and spirituality. Sip while celebrating the renewal of springtime or as a reminder to savor the season and celebrate the beautiful, fleeting moments of life.

SERVES 1

1 ounce freshly squeezed grapefruit juice for purification and positivity

1½ ounces Rose Tea (page 200 in the appendix) for love and beauty

¼ ounce agave for youth

¼ ounce yuzu juice + ¼ ounce more agave (optional but recommended)

½ teaspoon sakura blossom powder for renewal and beauty

Edible flower or cherry, for garnish

1. In your shaker, place the grapefruit juice, enjoying its uplifting and rejuvenating scent. Add the tea for love and healing.
2. Lightly sweeten with the agave, another blooming reminder of death and the temporary nature of life (see "Beyond the Glass" from the Moon Goddess Colada in chapter 8). Add the yuzu juice and additional agave, if using.
3. Sprinkle in the sakura powder—a symbol of beauty but also of the temporary nature of life. How are you going to celebrate and honor the moment?
4. Add ice and shake.
5. Strain into stemmed glassware and garnish. Say any affirmation that appeals to you for this moment while sipping the drink.

BEYOND THE GLASS

In Japan, sakura (cherry) blossom season runs between January and April. While the blossoms symbolize beauty, they are also a reminder of renewal and our mortality—to capture and celebrate the fleeting moments of life,[9] for the blossoming of a flower is only temporary. As you sip this recipe, reflect on the magic of this (or any) flower: How can you celebrate the beauty of the moment? How can you honor this fleeting renewal and new beginning?

ZERO-PROOF CANDLEMAS COCKTAIL

Hope, Cleansing, Spirituality

Nurture your inner hope with this zero-proof citrus, cream, and rosemary mocktail. More known by its alternate name, Imbolc, Candlemas is a day celebrated midway between the winter solstice and spring equinox in modern Wheel of the Year practices. It is a day of purification and cleansing, when candles are lit in a symbol of hope and to beacon back the spring after winter. Rosemary acts as the drink's "wick" and purifies, while cream soothes and orange blossom uplifts with its floral, jovial essence. You can use coconut milk for the nurturing energy of the hopeful crescent moon or add egg white to balance the citrus and symbolize rebirth. Made to appear like its namesake (a candle), this creamy vanilla and orange blossom recipe will cleanse energy and renew hope, whether you're preparing for the coming spring or just in need of some nurturing.

Orange blossom water is available online and in many stores with Mediterranean foods. Lyre's is available online as well.

SERVES 1

AFFIRMATIONS TO SIP BY:

I calm, soothe, and renew my spirit with each sip.

I trust my inner hope, like a budding candle flame, to guide the way.

Just like the hours of daylight grow from winter to spring, light also grows within.

BEYOND THE GLASS

Candle magic exists across cultures—from lighting candles in churches or at memorials to the ones on a witch's altar. They illuminate the darkness and are a symbol of hope and cleansing. Relate the symbolism of this drink to an actual candle to relight hope in your life. To do so, take a white candle and hold it in your hands. Think on what you are renewing in your life—whether it be hope or a specific intention you wish to nurture. Light the candle and while it burns, enjoy your mocktail, noting the resonance between the candle flame burning by you and the one growing in your belly, nurtured by each sip of this drink. Breathe deeply.

recipe continued on page 42

2 sprigs rosemary, divided for purification, peace, and insight

3–4 drops nonalcoholic lavender bitters (such as All The Bitter), or ¼ tsp dried lavender for purification and peace

1 ounce Honey Syrup (page 199 in the appendix) for spirituality and soothing

¼ teaspoon orange blossom/flower water

¼ teaspoon vanilla extract for peace

1 ounce freshly squeezed lemon juice for joy and purification

½–¾ ounce cream (such as half-and-half or coconut milk) for nurturing

½ ounce Lyre's Orange Sec (optional)

1 ounce Lyre's Dry London Spirit (optional)

1 egg white (optional) for rebirth and cleansing

1 Optional: Prepare the rosemary "wick": In a freezer-safe glass, place ~1 inch water. Stand 1 rosemary sprig upright, so that the stem rests in the water and the leaves poke above the lip of the glass. If desired, you can use butcher's twine tied to the rosemary and draped over the lips of the glass and a rubber band around the glass to hold the rosemary perfectly in the center. Set the glass in the freezer, keeping the rosemary in place, until the water is frozen.

2 In your shaker, add the remaining rosemary sprig for purification, the bitters for peace, and the soothing honey syrup. Add the orange blossom water and vanilla for peace. Add the lemon juice, reflecting on its cleansing and brightening energy—yellow like a candle's flame.

3 Add the cream for nurturing as well as any nonalcoholic subs, if using.

4 To add egg white to your drink, crack the egg while thinking of what you are rebirthing in your life. Then separate the white from the yolk and add the egg white to the drink. Shake twice: first without ice, then a second time with ice. If not using egg white, shaking once with ice should work fine.

5 Remove the frozen glass with the rosemary "wick" and strain the drink around the rosemary. Above the foam of the drink, the rosemary should poke up—a little green candle wick for cleansing and new beginnings.

6 For added affect, you can take a match (with caution) to the rosemary and light it while thinking on what you are cleansing, renewing, and bringing hope for. Since the rosemary is fresh, the flame should quickly go out but leave a little cleansing smoke. Say any affirmation that resonates with you while lighting the candle or while sipping.

ENERGETIC POTENTIAL OF SALT

When you think of cleansing spells and moon rituals, an earthy, luxurious herbal salt bath or a protective circle of salt might be the first thing that comes to mind. It's true—this ingredient has many magical applications, whether it be for protection, purification, or grounding. But it's also an important part of mixology, and that makes it the perfect opportunity to meld more magic into your mocktails. Learn about the magic of salt in your recipes and how to align the salt used in your drinks to your intention or even an aligned ritual to enhance the experience of your mocktail potions.

SALT MAGIC

In magic, salt is often used for purification, protection, repelling, or even connecting to the element of earth.

EARTH ELEMENT AND GROUNDING: On altars, salt is often placed in a dish to represent the earth element. With its connection to the earth, it is grounding in both flavor and energy.

PURIFICATION AND CLEANSING: A common use for salt in witchcraft is purification, akin to salt's antimicrobial properties. It is employed in cleansing bath salt recipes bolstered with cleansing herbs or added to floor washes and mixed with water in asperging rituals (sprinkled around the home) for purification and blessings.

PROTECTION AND DISPELLING: One of the most important uses for salt in magic is protection, and it is often sprinkled in a circle as an energetic barrier, mixed with fortifying herbs to place around the home, or added to protective witch bottles. Some mystics even place a small circle of salt around their spell candles to protect them from the influence of others.

TYPES OF SALT

Salt comes in an array of colors beyond your classic white table salt: pink, red, black, brown. Each has a slightly different flavor and essence. Of course, always use what is accessible to you, but when you're ready, invite yourself to explore the subtle nuances of various worldly salts.

BLACK LAVA SALT (food-grade) is different from what you buy at your local witch shop, so BE careful! The black salt sold at an occult or metaphysical shop is usually mixed with non–food safe items, such as ashes or toxic herbs. In comparison, black *lava* salt is specifically food-grade. It is known for its distinctive color and often comes from Hawaii or Cypress. A combination of sea salt and activated charcoal, it has a slight earthy and smoky flavor profile and is perfect for protection and detoxification magic. (Note that activated charcoal can interfere with certain medications. The amount ingested through a salt rim may be minimal, but always research beforehand to be safe.)

INDIAN BLACK SALT (also called Himalayan black salt) is a bit different—it is not black but more purplish–light gray. It contains trace amounts of sulfuric components, which give it an egg-like flavor and make it powerful in potions for dispelling unwanted energy or people.

HIMALAYAN SALT is known for its gentle pink-orange color, which comes from its iron content. It comes primarily from the Himalayas in Pakistan and is subtler in flavor. I personally like to use this salt for drinks with more of a healing nature, because of its more gentle, soothing essence.

SEA SALT is collected from evaporated seawater, often retaining minerals and other impurities from the ocean where it originates. Thus, its essence can vary significantly based on locality. Magically, I like to incorporate sea salt for cleansing, purifying, and renewing ocean energy and lunar potions.

SEASONED SALTS (such as celery salt) are popular as rims for drinks like the Bloody Mary. A mixture of salt with other herbal ingredients, they carry the potential to further attune your magical intentions to your drinks. For example, mixing with cayenne can be great for dispelling, whereas mixing with black pepper is protective and grounding.

SMOKED SALTS are produced by smoking the salt over a wood fire for a long length of time. It lends a smoky essence to your recipes, cultivating dispelling but also protective fiery energy. A pinch of it can also help produce the smoky essence of mezcal or scotch in mocktails.

USES IN MIXOLOGY

It's hard to imagine a margarita or paloma without salt. While the focus in mixology is often on syrups and sugars, salt is a just as important part of mixology. Flavor-wise, it can create a contrast to the sweetness of a recipe, enhance flavors, or even add electrolytes to water. Here's how you can employ the magic of salts in your mystical mocktails.

- **SALT RIMS**—Adhering a layer of salt on the edge of the glass's lip that starts the sipping experience of the drink.

  To rim a drink: Wet the outer edge of the lip of a glass with a citrus wedge. Pour salt in a dish and press the wetted rim into the salt. Different granule sizes of salt may stick easier or harder, but the liquid on the glass should hold the salt to the rim. Make sure you have enough juice and repeat if needed. If it looks messy, you can always clean the rim with a napkin. A good practice is to rim half the glass, so that you or your company has the option to alternate sips with or without salt.

- **SALINE SOLUTION**—While a rim may be the more familiar imagery of salt in mixology, another potent use is the crafting of a saline solution: 20 g salt to 80 g hot water. Dissolving salt into water to create a saline solution better integrates the benefits and flavor balance of salt when mixing into your mocktail. Using a saline solution can help bring out hidden flavors, enhance the sweetness, or balance citrus. Only a few drops are needed for a recipe.

- **ADDING A PINCH**—Last but not least, you can always just add a pinch directly to your drink! Beware, though: salt becomes more obvious in mocktails. So lean on the overcautious side when adding—you can always add more, but once mixed in, you can never detract!

ALIGNED RITUALS

Becoming aware of the potential magic and meaning of salt in your drinks can elevate the success of your potions. For example, relax in a cleansing salt bath while sipping on your cleansing nonalcoholic margarita for inner and outer purification. Or cast a spell for protection with a salt circle while sipping on a mocktail with a protective black salt rim. It's as simple as intentionally utilizing a salt rim on your mocktail and adding a pinch in your bath. Here are some other uses of salt in magic to get your ideas flowing for an aligned salt-based ritual to enjoy alongside your drink.

CLEANSE YOUR CRYSTALS: You can cleanse your crystals in a mixture of salt and water (just make sure the crystals aren't water soluble or softer than 4 on the Mohs hardness scale).

SALT BLEND: Craft a salt blend with herbs matching those in your mocktail to then use in spells as a candle dressing or as a protective barrier when sprinkled.

SALT BATH: Enjoy a basic salt bath or craft a special blend and soak in it while enjoying your drink for inner and outer purification!

SALT SCRUB: Craft a corresponding salt scrub with your drink, perfect for cleansing and renewing your energy with each scrub.

WITCH PROTECTION BOTTLE: Craft a witch bottle with a salt mixture for protection.

CONNECT TO THE EARTH ELEMENT: Place salt in a bowl on an altar to symbolize the earth.

CLEANSING THE HOME:

- Add a pinch to your floor wash or laundry for cleansing.
- Add a pinch to water to asperge the home (sprinkling around the home, such as with rosemary, for cleansing).
- Place a pinch of salt in the corners of the home for protection.

AFFIRMATIONS TO SIP BY:
I detoxify my energy of what no longer serves me.
I embrace the power of my pure essence.
My spirit is rejuvenated and fortified.

PURIFYING PALOMA

Rejuvenation, Purification, Hex-Breaking

Get energy moving and cleanse with this zesty jalapeño and almond paloma. A spicy nonalcoholic twist on the traditional paloma, this elixir will help to purify, detox, and fortify your energy—perfect for clearing through blockages and energizing your system to move forward with success. Jalapeño and lime will dispel any ill will getting in your way, while rejuvenating kumquat, grapefruit, and orgeat (an almond and orange blossom syrup available at mixology stores or online) will bring renewal and healing.

SERVES 1

Sea salt, for rim for cleansing

2 slices kumquat (optional) for luck

2–3 slices jalapeño for moving energy

½ ounce orgeat for healing **(or ¼ agave syrup)**

3 drops nonalcoholic aromatic bitters (such as All The Bitter) (optional)

½ ounce freshly squeezed lime juice for healing and hex-breaking

1 ounce freshly squeezed grapefruit juice for purification and positivity

1 ounce soda water

Mint sprig and grapefruit wedge, for garnish

1 Rim a glass halfway with sea salt—a protective circle of salt around your glass to cleanse your energy.

2 In your glass, add the optional kumquat for rejuvenation and the jalapeño to get things moving. Add orgeat for healing and the bitters, if using, for the fortifying energy of numerous herbs. Muddle.

3 Pour in the lime and grapefruit juices to cleanse and uplift, then add ice and top with bubbly soda water to raise your energy.

4 Garnish with a slapped mint sprig and/or grapefruit wedge to renew your mind with its scent upon each sip. As needed, squeeze the grapefruit while thinking on what you're purifying.

BEYOND THE GLASS

Nothing cleanses quite like selenite. Renew your energy and reconnect to your spiritual center with this stone. A crystal associated with purifying energy and the "higher self" (a transcendent part of your being that's free from ego), selenite is the perfect accompaniment to this drink. While enjoying the drink, wave a selenite stick around your body and through your energy field, helping dispel any further unwanted energy from your aura in perfect resonance with the drink.

AFFIRMATIONS TO SIP BY:
Blockages clear from my way with ease.
The doors of opportunity are open to me.
I am open to new possibilities and paths.

Mango and Mandarin Road-Opening Mocktail

Vitality, Changing Luck, Success

Break through blockages and open the pathway to success with this mandarin and mango frozen mocktail. Sometimes when things feel stuck in life, you need just a bit of a breakthrough. With turmeric to purify, ginger for success, and yuzu for renewal, this is just the elixir you need to pave a new way forward. Lemongrass will bring good luck, and mango and mandarin (often used as an offering to deities) will help bring blessings for prosperity. A sip of this and you will feel new doors opening for you in no time!

SERVES 1

1 slice fresh ginger, or pinch of ground turmeric for clearing the way

2–4 mint leaves for refreshing the mind

¼ ounce Lemongrass Simple Syrup (page 199 in the appendix), or classic simple syrup for good luck

¼ cup mango for prosperity

½–1 cup ice

1 ounce freshly squeezed mandarin or orange juice for luck

½ ounce yuzu juice, or 1 ounce freshly squeezed lemon juice for rejuvenation

½ ounce Lyre's Orange Sec (optional)

1 ounce Lyre's White Cane Spirit (optional)

Mint sprig or fresh bay leaf, for garnish

1. In a blender, place all the ingredients. If adding nonalcoholic spirits, you may need to add more ice. Do so, then blend—envisioning blockages breaking down like the blender breaks down the ice and ingredients.

2. Pour the mixture into a coupe and garnish with a mint sprig to clear your senses with each sip or a bay leaf for blessings and wishes. As you taste, tune in to the revitalizing energy of the recipe and say any affirmations that appeal to you.

Beyond the Glass

The crescent moon is a symbol of hope. A little sliver of the moon visible in the sky, just starting to grow to full; it is at the very start of its journey. With the moon not fully or even halfway lit, it is a reminder (1) to not give up when the journey has just begun, and (2) that not all the factors are decided or illuminated just yet. Through opening your energy to new possibilities and pathways, you can still determine the outcome of your endeavor. When the road seems blocked, ask yourself what alternative pathways you can explore to reach your goals. What knowledge or factors can be illuminated to help you pave the way forward? Invite this insight into your consciousness.

AFFIRMATIONS TO SIP BY:

I am divinely protected.

I am grounded in my body and experience.

I set boundaries with confidence and ease.

COSMO-CALLY® PROTECTED

Protection, Clearing, Boundaries

Imbue your energy with an aura of protection with this cleansing rosemary and cranberry nonalcoholic cosmo. With antioxidant-rich blackberry, grounding black pepper, and cleansing rosemary, this recipe is loaded with not just ingredients good for immunity but also ones associated with psychic protection, energetic cleansing, and boundaries in modern Western magic. Whether looking for a sip to detoxify after an unwanted encounter or setting energetic boundaries, this Cosmo-cally Protected free-spirited cocktail has your back.

SERVES 1

Black Hawaiian lava salt or sugar, for rim (optional)

6 blueberries for psychic protection

2 rosemary sprigs, separated, for purification

⅛ teaspoon ground black pepper for dispelling and protection

½ ounce agave (or 1 ounce Lavender-Agave Syrup, see appendix)

1 ounce freshly squeezed lime juice for hex-breaking

⅔ ounce cranberry juice for protection and action

1 ounce soda water

1. For an extra protective addition, rim a martini glass with food-grade black lava salt (see "Salt" section for how to rim a glass) or black sugar.
2. In your shaker, place the blueberries for psychic protection and one rosemary sprig. Sprinkle in the grounding black pepper and agave. Muddle the rosemary and blueberries into the agave, envisioning putting down firm boundaries—symbolically putting your foot down. Say any of the affirmations now, if desired.
3. Add the purifying lime juice and pour in the protective cranberry juice.
4. Add ice, shake, and strain into your martini glass.
5. Top with soda water and garnish with the remaining rosemary sprig (you can lightly set aflame the outer leaves with a match for cleansing smoke) to purify and uplift the mind with each sip.

BEYOND THE GLASS

Just like you might drink cranberry juice to boost your immune system (your internal "protection" system), it's also associated with protection in magic. In fact, the holiday tradition of stringing cranberries makes a great protective craft! Associated with Mars and the element of fire, cranberry helps to embolden goals, action, and passion. As a berry, it can also be associated with abundance—showcasing that protecting one's energy is part of cultivating fruitful efforts.

AFFIRMATIONS TO SIP BY:
Connected to Mother Earth, I am revitalized and energized.
I release limitations and embrace positive energy.
I'm a magnet for good luck and good vibes.

YERBA MATÉ MOCKTAIL

Purification, Energy, Luck

Connect to the earth and purify your energy of psychic debris with this lemongrass Yerba Maté no-jito. (If lemongrass isn't available for this recipe, feel free to substitute with classic simple syrup or agave, or even the lavender-agave syrup in the appendix.) Yerba maté has many benefits, and, lightly caffeinated, it can be just what you need to put some pep in your step. With its earthy aroma combined with energizing citrus and refreshing mint, this Yerba Maté Mocktail will invigorate your senses. Imbibe when needing to purify and change your luck or energize your body and mind.

SERVES 1–2

2 sprigs thyme for purification and courage

3–5 leaves mint for refreshing the mind

2 drops nonalcoholic lavender bitters (such as All The Bitter) (optional) for peace

1 ounce Lemongrass Simple Syrup (page 199 in the appendix) or ½–1 ounce agave for purification and changing luck

3 ounces Yerba Maté (page 200 in the appendix) for energy and earth connection

½ ounce freshly squeezed lime juice for clearing hexes

1 ounce tonic water

Extra thyme and/or mint sprig, for garnish

1. In the bottom of your glass, place the thyme for purification and fortifying energy, and the mint to cleanse the mind. Add the bitters for peace and syrup of choice.

2. Muddle the mint and thyme into the syrup, infusing their purifying aromas together, while saying any affirmation or intention that appeals to you.

3. Add the yerba maté for vitality, then add ice. Top with the cleansing lime juice and tonic water. Give it a quick stir and garnish with an extra thyme and/or mint sprig to greet the nose with some aromatic magic upon each sip.

BEYOND THE GLASS

Grounding refers to connecting to the earth. Through a variety of meditations or techniques, grounding can help one feel more in their body and be focused on the present moment. It can also help neutralize energy and boost vitality toward your endeavors, giving renewed energy and direction. Complement this drink by connecting to the earth, such as standing barefoot or whatever method speaks to you. With each sip, breathe deeply and bring your awareness to your feet. You might recall the traditions you learned in chapter 1. Give thanks for the gift of this sacred herb and connect in gratitude to Mother Earth.

AFFIRMATIONS TO SIP BY:

My mind is clear and calm.

With each sip, I uplift my thoughts.

Like the gentle sea breeze for which it is named, rosemary clears my senses.

CLEAR MIND MINT JULEP

Focus, Clarity, Cleansing

Inspire clarity and free your mind with this minty rosemary and white tea recipe. Bolstered with grapefruit and agave, this nonalcoholic mint julep is perfect for elevating your spirit (and your thoughts) after a long and tiresome day. Mint clears and calms, while a hidden touch of salt grounds and purifies. With the magic of rosemary and white tea, your cognitive senses will feel rejuvenated, allowing you to unwind and focus your energy in other ways. This is just the recipe to bring peace to the body and mind when you need something simple and refreshing.

SERVES 1

2 sprigs rosemary, separated

3–5 mint leaves for mental abilities and calming

¼ ounce agave

Pinch of sea salt for grounding and purification

1 ounce freshly squeezed grapefruit juice for purification and positivity

1½ ounces White Tea (page 200 in the appendix) for the conscious mind

2 ounces soda water

1. Add one of the rosemary sprigs and the mint to your glass, breathing in their aroma and oils. Add the agave and lightly muddle, stamping out any stressful thoughts. Say any affirmations that appeal to you at this time.
2. Sprinkle the salt for grounding and purification and add the grapefruit juice for cleansing and positivity.
3. Add shaved or crushed ice to your glass and pour in the tea to elevate your conscious mind. Top with the soda water.
4. Garnish with the remaining rosemary sprig to clear your mind with each sip.

BEYOND THE GLASS

What better ingredient to use to calm, cleanse, and bring peace to the mind than fresh garden rosemary? Rosemary's scientific name, *Rosmarinus*, means "dew of the sea," for the Mediterranean cliffs upon which it grows. Oftentimes, just the scent of this evergreen shrub is relaxing and invigorating—rosemary has been shown to help enhance the mind and memory,[6] and its scent (reminiscent of the seaside after which it is named) often brings peace and relaxation. An especially magical herb, this shrub is often used for the mind, peace, purification, protection, healing, and enhancing psychic insight in witchcraft practices. A sprig of this to greet the nose with each sip will do wonders to help unwind the mind!

AFFIRMATIONS TO SIP BY:
I release the energy or words of others.
I cleanse what does not serve me.
I reclaim and stand in my power.

SMOKE AND FIRE

Hex-Breaking, Protection, Purification

Where there's smoke, there's fire. While we do our best to be positive and surround ourselves with support, there come times when we need to dispel the negative energy of others. With ingredients to cleanse and unhex, this smoky and spicy recipe has what you need to purify so you can keep carrying on. The fresh bit of ginger (along with lime) helps energy move and reclaim your inner power, while salt sets some solid boundaries. Sip when you need to remove some blockages, serve to dispel negativity, or enjoy just when you want to shake something off.

SERVES 1

Smoked or black Indian salt, for rim

2 slices fresh ginger for power

3 sage leaves for purification

⅛ tsp ground cayenne for hex-breaking

½ ounce agave

Pinch of smoked salt or pinch of salt + dash of liquid smoke for grounding and protection

¾ ounce freshly squeezed lime juice for protection and hex-breaking

1½ ounces cranberry juice for protection and action

½ ounce Lyre's Orange sec or freshly squeezed orange juice

1½ ounces nonalcoholic tequila replacement or soda water (optional)

Sage sprig, for garnish

1. Rim a glass with a mixture of your choice of black lava or smoked salt.
2. In your shaker, place the ginger for power, the sage for purification, and the cayenne to dispel hexes.
3. Add the agave, then muddle the fresh ingredients—visualizing stamping down and out the words of others. Say any affirmations now.
4. Add a pinch of salt to ground and set boundaries and the smoked salt for smoky fire energy.
5. Add the lime juice, the cranberry juice for protection, as well as any nonalcoholic spirits. If adding fresh orange juice, add extra lime to taste to rebalance any extra sweetness.
6. Add ice and shake. As you do so, use the opportunity of shaking to "shake" off the energy of others.
7. Pour into your glass and garnish. Lightly smoke the sage sprig to cleanse your energy.

BEYOND THE GLASS

Match the energy and the namesake of this mocktail by tapping into the power of smoky quartz. This stone helps to filter out the energy of others while keeping yours grounded and clear. When flaming the fresh sage, brush the crystal through the smoke and envision a protective haze surrounding you, setting a boundary.

HERBAL CLEANSING BUNDLES

Mystical drink-making often calls for fresh and powerful herbs. Many, such as rosemary or thyme, also have numerous uses in spells and rituals. When buying these herbs for drink recipes, however, there may be too much to reasonably use before they go bad. Alternatively, you may even feel a tad wasteful throwing away that used rosemary sprig in the bottom of your cocktail or garnish left over in your glass. While its flavor may have been incorporated into a drink, you can still reuse it for spiritual and ritual purposes.

One way I like to reuse and create greater resonance with the magic of recipes is through crafting smoke-cleansing bundles. In witchcraft, smoke-cleansing bundles are a popular way to burn herbs for purification and cleansing. Through crafting your own from culinary herbs, you not only prevent unnecessary waste but also create the opportunity to prolong your magic. For example, you can make the Cosmo-cally Protected and then use any leftover rosemary for a cleansing bundle. This means collecting the sprigs left in the bottom of your shaker and rinsing them or using extra herbs before they go bad. But through cleaning them, removing any water, binding them with twine, and drying them, you can create your own smoke-cleansing bundles.

Here are a few herbs we use in mixology that can be used for such purposes and how to craft your own bundles:

BAY LEAF: **Dreams, Healing, Protection, Prophecy, Purification, Strength, Success, Wishes, Wisdom**

Bay leaves have numerous uses in magic: They are used for making wishes and burned for psychic powers, for divine wisdom or purification, and even as a symbol of success and victory. You can find them dried in the spice aisle, but you'll want them fresh for bundles or else they may break. Luckily, many grocery stores carry them in the produce section. Because these aren't long twigs like rosemary, I usually use them as the outer layer of an herb bundle. They can be more challenging to bind, so tuck them under the twine as you wrap upward.

ROSEMARY: Healing, Love, the Mind, Peace, Protection, Purification, Sleep
Associated in magical folklore with the element of air (and with a name meaning "dew of the sea"), the scent of this Mediterranean herb is often used to enhance memory and relax the mind. It is also a popular herb to burn for cleansing, to dispel nightmares, or to open the mind to spiritual knowledge. This one naturally lends itself to cleansing bundles of all kinds.

THYME: Courage, Healing, Love, Purification, Psychic Abilities, Strength, Sleep
Thyme is often burned for good health, which is why I love to incorporate it into cleansing bundles to prepare a space for healing or energy work. Like rosemary, it also aids peaceful rest and psychic abilities. It is associated with courage, energy, and the fae. Altogether, it can be peaceful to the mind yet healing and fortifying to the body in cleansing bundles—perfect for healing work and health magic.

GARDEN/CULINARY SAGE: Focus, Health, Longevity, Purification, Wisdom, Spirit
It is important to distinguish sage fresh from the grocery store for cooking from white sage and "smudging"—smudging is a closed Native American practice, and the cultural appropriation of it has led to overharvesting, making it less accessible for many natives.

The sage we use in this book—culinary sage—is what you find at the grocery store in the produce section and is specifically grown and cultivated for cooking. Sage is a great herb for purification but also for longevity, focus, and spiritual knowledge. Alongside rosemary, it can be great to burn for the mind and to glean spiritual information.

CRAFTING A CLEANSING BUNDLE

Through finding ways to reuse the herbs you use in your drinks for spiritual purposes, you not only feel a bit better about waste but also can create herb bundles corresponding to what you are imbibing. You can combine various herbs and create unique bundles with different scents and energy that echo what you are working on in your life.

HERE'S HOW TO BIND A CLEANSING BUNDLE:

1. If used in a recipe, wash and pat dry. If it was boiled and the stem soaked over a long period of time, you may need to let it dry a bit. Gather twine, scissors, and your herbs.

2. Arrange your herbs so that their stems are aligned. You can also layer and incorporate several herbs together. For example, an inner layer of thyme, then rosemary, then an exterior of bay leaf.

3. Tie the stems together with twine, leaving plenty of string on both ends for you to weave up and down the bundle.

4. Wrap both ends of the twine around and up the bundle, holding it tightly as you crisscross the strings. You may also knot the strings in a couple of spots to stabilize the binding.

5. If incorporating leaves like bay leaves or large organic rose petals, you will need to tuck them in under each binding as you move up.

6. Once you get to the top, knot and wind it back down to the stem. Here you can tie a final knot and cut the string.

7. Hang it up to dry upside down for 1–2 weeks. For added energy, charge under the waning moon.

TO BURN: Unravel some of the twine a safe distance from the tip of the bundle. Over a dish, light the end on fire and then blow out the flame. The smoke produced from the embers is the cleansing smoke. Keeping it on the dish, you can waft the cleansing smoke to any area you wish to purify or bless with its energy.

AFFIRMATIONS TO SIP BY:

My spirit is filled with renewal.

I am blossoming with positivity within every part of my being.

I cultivate more joy in my life.

FREE-SPIRITED LAVENDER LIMONCELLO

Renewal, Cleansing, Joy

Few combinations are as iconic and memorable as lavender and lemon. In this sans-alcohol rendition of homemade limoncello, brightening citrus pairs with peace-inspiring lavender to foster your inner sense of joy. Whether you're celebrating spring or encouraging that bright sense of optimism and renewal that the season brings within, this reviving recipe will have you feeling radiant and uplifted to step forward on a new path.

SERVES 4–6

Peel of 2 lemons

½ cup sugar

½–1 tablespoon dried lavender

½ cup hot water

6–9 ounces freshly squeezed lemon juice

6 ounces nonalcoholic sparkling white wine or 12 ounces soda water

Lavender sprig or lemon peel twist, for garnish

1. Peel the lemons. Place the peels in an airtight jar, cover with the sugar, and shake.
2. Let the mixture sit for 24–48 hours, shaking occasionally. The oils will mix with the sugar and form an oleo-saccharum.
3. In the same jar, add the lavender to the mixture and pour in the hot water. Steep for 5–10 minutes, then strain.
4. This should yield about ¾ cup syrup, which is about 6 ounces. Transfer to a pitcher and add the lemon juice, to taste. Top with the sparkling wine or soda water. Alternatively, if making individual servings, measure 1 ounce cordial to 1–1 ½ ounces lemon juice, to 1 ounce nonalcoholic sparkling white wine or 2 ounces soda water.
5. Pour into champagne glasses and garnish.

BEYOND THE GLASS

Ostara, the celebration of the vernal equinox, celebrates the first day of spring. Coming from winter, when we rested, and Imbolc, when we fostered hope, spring offers the joyful, abundant energy and the revival of life. It is a time of renewal, optimism, and growth. While the spring equinox also brings a day of temporary balance between hours of daylight and hours of dark, the hours of daylight will continue to grow. As you sip (and maybe share) this concoction, ask yourself: How will you find joy and renewal? Like the vibrant lemon and peaceful lavender of this recipe, how can you foster rejuvenation and peace within your spirit?

AFFIRMATIONS TO SIP BY:
I elevate my mind and energy to a higher awareness.
The way is open for new ideas and new beginnings.
I am ready for new possibilities.

RENEWING YUZU SOUR

Rejuvenation, Awakening, the Conscious Mind

Bring peace of mind and elevate your consciousness with this cucumber and mint Renewing Yuzu Sour. This revitalizing, awakening recipe features the restorative properties of cucumber and the mind-clearing and calming energy of lavender and mint. Yuzu (easily purchased online) awakens your inner spirit, bringing a citrus essence along with grapefruit to boost your mood. Sweetened with an easily homemade jasmine green tea syrup for the conscious mind and spiritual elevation, this recipe is a great complement for refreshing your mind or energy, or even springtime celebrations.

SERVES 1

2 slices cucumber for rejuvenation

1 sprig mint for calm, refreshing the mind

¾ ounce Jasmine Green Tea Syrup (page 199 in the appendix) for the conscious mind and spiritual elevation

4 drops nonalcoholic lavender bitters (such as All The Bitter) for peace and purification

½ ounce yuzu juice for renewal, awakening, and resilience

½ ounce freshly squeezed grapefruit juice for purification and positivity

1½ ounce Seedlip Garden 108 or soda water

½ ounce Lyre's Orange Sec for inspiration, creativity, joy

Cucumber peel and mint sprig, for garnish

1 In your shaker, place the cucumber. Breathe in the refreshing scent of the mint to uplift your mind, then add it to the shaker.

2 Pour in the syrup, the bitters for peace, the yuzu for awakening, and the grapefruit juice for purification.

3 Add in any nonalcoholic spirits. If using soda water, save it for the end. Add ice, then shake.

4 Double strain into a coupe. Add the soda water now, if using.

5 Slap the mint to activate its oils and place it as garnish, alongside a cucumber sliver. Sip, then say any affirmation that resonates, feeling the clearing energy of this recipe open your mind to higher consciousness.

BEYOND THE GLASS

Yuzu is a citrus, often described as a mix between a mandarin and a lemon. In Edo period Japan, yuzu would be added to winter solstice baths. It would also be given for prosperity and good luck. Altogether, it is a great citrus to add rejuvenation, relaxation, and luck to your recipes and also to utilize some citrus other than the usual lemon or lime. While it may seem exotic, it is very easy to purchase 100% yuzu juice online (one bottle will often go a long a way since the flavor is so condensed) or in Asian markets.

AFFIRMATIONS TO SIP BY:

I shake away any unwanted energy.

My spirit is rejuvenated.

I celebrate the magic in every moment.

MAGICAL MARGARITA(S)

Cleansing, Purification, Luck

Practical Magic is one of those movies that left its mark on many mystical people—especially the "Midnight Margaritas" scene. Now you can re-create the magic of that moment without the alcohol. With ingredients from hidden gems in the movie, like lavender for luck, salt, rosemary, lime for unhexing, and of course coconut, this is a drink for cleansing, luck, and good vibes. This hydrating and zesty nonalcoholic margarita is the perfect recipe to clear away the blues and revive your spirit or, like the Owens sisters, break generational curses and fall in love with life.

You can buy Lyre's Orange Sec online or in stores.

SERVES 1

Sea salt or sugar and ground rosemary or lavender, for rim (optional)

1 sprig rosemary for remembrance, purification, and peace

Pinch of salt for grounding, protection, and purification

1 ounce Lavender-Agave Syrup (page 199 in the appendix) for love, purification, and peace

½ ounce freshly squeezed lime juice for hex-breaking

½ ounce coconut water for inner purification and psychic awareness

½ ounce orange juice or Lyre's Orange Sec for luck and inspiration

1 ounce soda water or nonalcoholic tequila substitute

Lavender or rosemary sprig, for garnish

1 Mix your choice of salt or sugar with powdered rosemary or lavender (you can powder it yourself in a coffee grinder). Rim the edge of your glass as instructed in chapter 4.

2 In your shaker, place the rosemary while breathing in its magical aroma to uplift and clear the mind.

3 Add the salt for grounding and the syrup. Add the lime juice, having squeezed away any unwanted energy or hexes. Say any affirmations at this time.

4 Add the coconut water for internal purification and, of course, any margarita needs a bit of orange juice for luck.

5 Add ice and shake. Pour into the rimmed glass, top with soda water, if using, and garnish.

BEYOND THE GLASS

In the "Midnight Margaritas" scene, the Owens family is dancing around a table. Letting your body move and stepping into this moment of magic can help you "shake off" unwanted energy and reinvigorate your spirit. As you shake this drink, channel your inner Owens family energy and allow yourself to dance a bit—it will help shift your energy and infuse the moment with your intention.

CHAPTER 6

CONNECTION

Potions for Friendship, Family, and Romance

From meeting at coffee shops to congregating in bars, drinks are often the social lubricant for how we connect and exchange energy. But they don't need to be centered around alcohol. In this chapter, you will find 12 beverages to inspire connection, warmth, and harmony. Melt hearts with the zesty Rose and Maple Frozen (nonalcoholic) Daiquiri, using rose tea ice cubes to invite love. Reconcile and invite compassion in a difficult relationship with the Compassion Mocktail, using basil to soften resentment and open the heart. The drinks you serve don't have to be about a momentary high but rather can be a vehicle for healing and authentic connections.

The following recipes invite you on a journey to sip in harmony, love, and empathy of all kinds—whether with friends, family, or coworkers, or even just feeling connected to the greater universe. Since sharing drinks can often mean a gathering, many of these recipes can be made in bulk. With insight on how to make magical and eye-catching ice cubes, prebatched drinks served over ice can be just as enchanting as freshly made mocktails.

From using lavender to keep the peace (and clear communication) or hibiscus for low blood pressure and zesty fun, you will glean how the right ingredients can invite good moods and help cultivate harmony, love, and connection. The "Affirmations to Sip By" with each recipe in this section can be used as toasts by swapping the "I" for "We," helping further your connection with one another. Lastly, when you're sharing a drink one-on-one, you'll learn how the right garnish can be an aromatizing spell in itself.

MAKING MAGICAL ICE CUBES

When it comes to serving guests, even something as enchanting as an ice cube can add a touch of magic. Water makes up a large part of cocktails and even more so mocktails. Especially when prebatching recipes for gatherings, ice is often the last step for serving. By energetically charging the water you'll use for cubes and freezing it with aligned items, you create not just eye-catching ice cubes but also a spell—as the ice melts in your guests' drinks, any iciness will dissipate and help them open up for connection. Here are some ways to enchant your ice cubes for your next gathering:

- **Moon-Charged**—You can charge the purified water you use for your ice cubes under the power of the moon! You can even get nuanced and examine the energy of a particular moon. This can be a great way to add a magical, healing element to recipes to be shared. The moon has a sacred connection to the element of water. To create moon water, charge (by leaving out, sealed) the water you're using for ice cubes under the moon at night. Remove first thing in the morning and freeze into ice cubes.
- **Sun-Charged**—Just like you can charge water with the moon, you can do so with the sun. Charging with the sun also adds the opportunity to infuse gentle herbal ingredients, such as fresh rose petals.

FREEZING GARNISHES

In addition to charging your water for ice cubes under the celestial energy of the moon or sun, you can also freeze items inside each one. Generally, I suggest freezing ingredients that are larger, as smaller flowers like chamomile might look pretty but will quickly become an annoyance floating around the drink as the ice melts.

LARGE ORGANIC ROSE PETALS: If you're lucky enough to have access to large, fresh organic roses, freezing their petals in spherical cubes has made some of the prettiest ice cubes I've ever seen. Their elegance is captured in time, and their color reflects magically in the cube. Roses are great for inspiring loving connection.

BUTTERFLY PEA FLOWER TEA: Like in the Moon Goddess Colada (in chapter 8), you can make a butterfly pea flower tea, which you then freeze. This deep blue ice cube will change the color of your drink as it diffuses, as butterfly pea flower changes color upon contact with acid. Butterfly pea flower ice cubes are great for not just dazzling but also adding peaceful, happy energy to a gathering. Just be aware that it is best to avoid butterfly pea flower if pregnant.

BERRIES: You can freeze berries for their various colors, flavors, and energy. Raspberries are great for happiness, blackberries for sensuality, blueberries for peace and protection, and strawberries for harmony and love.

CUCUMBER: Cucumber adds a calming, healing energy for peace to a gathering, and it can even be frozen into rose-like shapes. Freezing cucumber slices like the petals of a rose in a square cube can create that effect.

CITRUS: Similarly, you can also freeze citrus half moons into a rose or flower shape.

For more ice cube ideas for your magical mocktails, check out the Zero-Proof Candlemas Cocktail, Rose and Maple Frozen Daiquiri, or the Blessing Mimosa Bombs, all of which use freezing in unique ways for your mocktail recipes. As you can see, the possibilities are endless. Allow your creativity to soar as you mix and match these techniques to further imbue the magic of water into your mystical mocktails.

AFFIRMATIONS TO SIP BY:

I attract meaningful and exciting spiritual connections.

I embrace my sacred sensuality.

I am in tune with my passion, body, and spirit.

LUNAR PASSION

Passion, Healing, Spirituality, Happiness

Cooling coconut, tropical pineapple, and tangy hibiscus fan the flames of a spiritual love connection in this citrus mocktail. A mix of lunar and fiery ingredients, this tropical elixir will inspire deep conversation and passion—a perfect accent to a date night or to awakening your inner sensual, intuitive goddess. Grapefruit, lemon, and pineapple create a balance of tangy and tart flavors to uplift your energy, while coconut soothes, cools, and invites spiritual awareness. Topped with vibrant hibiscus tea, this visually stunning zero-proof cocktail has a layered effect to entice the eyes as equally as its flavor.

SERVES 1

Himalayan salt or sugar and dried hibiscus, for rim

½ ounce agave, plus more to taste

1 ounce freshly squeezed grapefruit juice for positivity

1 ounce coconut water or nonalcoholic coconut spirit (such as Beckett's or Caleño)

1 ounce freshly squeezed lemon juice

Pinch of ground cinnamon

1 ounce pineapple juice (optional but recommended) for hospitality

1 ounce nonalcoholic tequila replacement (such as Ritual) (optional)

1 ounce Hibiscus Tea (page 199 in the appendix) for sensuality

Dried edible flower, for garnish

1 On a plate, sprinkle the salt for grounding and healing (or sub sugar). Sprinkle the hibiscus and any other dried florals, mixing them into the granules. Rub a citrus slice against the side of your glass and press the glass into the mixture.

2 In your shaker, place the agave, grapefruit juice, coconut water, and lemon juice. Alternatively, you can build the drink directly in the glass, but be aware that the cinnamon may float around.

3 Sprinkle the cinnamon for spiritual elevation and lust, then add the pineapple juice for hospitality, and the tequila replacement, if using. Add ice and shake. As you shake your concoction, recite any affirmations that resonate with you.

4 Strain over ice into the finished glass. Top with a layer of vibrant hibiscus tea and garnish.

BEYOND THE GLASS

A spice associated with raising vibrational energy, fast luck, love, and lust, cinnamon is a perfect accent to this recipe and your magic. When sprinkled over a flame, ground cinnamon will also create sparks. For a little bit of love magic, you can sprinkle a tiny amount of ground cinnamon a safe distance above a candle flame and watch the sparks "fly."

AFFIRMATIONS TO SIP BY:
I attract joy and happiness in my friendships.
Joyful connections surround me.
I'm a magnet for supportive friendships.

SWEET PEACH SANS-GRIA

Friendship, Love, Happiness

There's nothing quite like a refreshing sangria to inspire fun and connection. With peach and maple, this white, nonalcoholic sangria recipe will sweeten hearts and inspire friendship. Ginger, lemon, and orange enliven positivity, while peach brings happiness. A sprinkle of cardamom invites love and mood-boosting, while maple allures. This sans-alcohol white sangria recipe is an enchanting spell to inspire friendship, love, and happiness. The recipe increments are to make one on demand, but you can multiply the recipe to make a full batch and infuse in the refrigerator to share at your next gathering. Instead of nonalcoholic white wine, you can use white grape juice and double the lemon from ½ to 1 ounce.

SERVES 1

1 slice fresh ginger for energy

2 slices fresh peach for love and happiness

½ ounce maple syrup for love

⅛ teaspoon ground cardamom for love

4 dashes nonalcoholic orange bitters or ½ ounce orange juice for joy

½ ounce freshly squeezed lemon juice for friendship and happiness

3 ounces nonalcoholic sauvignon blanc (white wine)

1 In your shaker, place the ginger for energy and the peaches for happiness. Add the syrup for love and attraction and muddle the ingredients while envisioning the dissolution of any barriers to connection.

2 Add the cardamom for love, the orange for brightening, and the lemon juice for friendship. Add the nonalcoholic wine and ice, then shake.

3 Pour into a wine glass and enjoy, saying any affirmations that appeal.

BEYOND THE GLASS

From the saying "sweet as a peach," you can imagine that this ingredient has a magical quality to attract. In fact, eating this fruit can help invite reciprocity in love or win over hearts. As you drink the fresh peach in this recipe, reflect on its energy. How can you allow for a freer flow of love and connection in your life?

AFFIRMATIONS TO SIP BY:
I neutralize negativity with each sip.
Harmony and positivity fill my relationships.
I am grounded with feel-good energy.

STRAWBERRY BALSAMIC BEVERAGE

Harmony, Grounding, Banishing Negativity

Cleanse bad vibes, rebalance, and promote harmony with this Strawberry Balsamic Beverage. This is a zesty elixir with strawberry for love and harmony, a perfect match flavor-wise for basil, which also brings love and helps banish negative energy. The flavors meld perfectly with a bit of balsamic vinegar to cleanse and rebalance the gut. This health tonic is perfect to complement some summer fun by grounding and removing negative energy between people. It's just the recipe to banish bad days while nurturing your body! For a larger size, double the ingredients.

SERVES 1

2 teaspoons balsamic vinegar for cleansing/banishing

2 strawberries for harmony and good luck

6 small basil leaves for love and banishing negative energy

2 slices fresh ginger for getting energy moving

1 ounce Honey Syrup (page 199 in the appendix) for soothing and purification

4 drops nonalcoholic lavender bitters (such as All The Bitter) (optional) for peace

2 ounces freshly squeezed grapefruit juice for purification and positivity

2 ounces soda water

Basil sprig with strawberry snack, for garnish

1. In your glass, place the vinegar—the cleansing base to the recipe to neutralize negative energy.
2. Add the strawberries for love and harmony. Atop, add the basil, ginger, and syrup to clear, energize, and soothe. Add optional lavender bitters.
3. Muddle these ingredients, saying the affirmations to claim your energy and intention for the recipe.
4. Add ice and grapefruit juice for positivity. Top with the soda water for some nice bubbles and garnish with a slapped basil sprig or leaf and a luscious strawberry for a happiness-inducing snack.

BEYOND THE GLASS

Strawberry is an ingredient associated with love, harmony, and good luck. It can help kindle friendship and stimulate love—it has become the iconic marker for Valentine's Day for this reason. In this recipe, strawberry helps to harmonize in the face of any potential negativity. If you know someone has ill will toward you, you can use a toothpick to engrave their name on the strawberry and, as you muddle, visualize stamping out any disdain so that they might open up to you.

AFFIRMATIONS TO SIP BY:
My love grows stronger each day.
I connect heart-to-heart, soul-to-soul in my relationships.
I cultivate happiness, fidelity, and trust.

MARRIAGE MOCKTAIL

Love, Fidelity, Happiness

Weddings are infamous for their drinking culture, but with nonalcoholic spirits, you can craft a perfect sober wedding drink to celebrate the occasion. Using ingredients associated with unions and marriage, this is a magical mocktail for love, fidelity, and happiness. Cardamom and nutmeg spice the recipe with love and fidelity, and peach brings happiness. The mocktail is sweetened with orgeat—an almond syrup reminiscent of the candied almonds used to celebrate weddings—and orange to bless unions for success.

SERVES 1

2 slices peach (optional) for love and happiness

2 cherries for happiness in marriage

1 ounce orgeat for wisdom and success

⅛ teaspoon ground cardamom for love

⅛ teaspoon ground nutmeg for fidelity

1 ounce freshly squeezed lemon juice for fidelity and friendship

½ ounce freshly squeezed orange juice for blessings

2 ounces nonalcoholic sparkling white wine to celebrate

Edible flower, for garnish

1. In your shaker, place the peach and cherry for love and happiness in union.
2. Add the orgeat for a successful union and muddle the ingredients.
3. Sprinkle the cardamom for love and the nutmeg for fidelity. Then, add the lemon and orange juice.
4. Add ice, shake, and strain into a coupe.
5. Top with the sparkling white wine and garnish.

BEYOND THE GLASS

Beltane marks the halfway point from spring to summer, mixing the renewal of spring with the fun of summer. From dancing around a maypole to jumping over fires, this day celebrates union and fertility. In fact, weddings on Beltane are a common tradition. Through unions the fertility of life is created. But it doesn't have to be about procreation—it can be about alchemy and how combining different elements can give way to new creations. Whether you're celebrating a marriage or just greater connection within yourself, what new life will be created?

AFFIRMATIONS TO SIP BY:
My heart opens and connects in authenticity.
I resolve old issues and mend my spirit.
I embrace compassion for myself and others.

COMPASSION CONCOCTION

Compassion, Peace, Healing

Clear the way for connection and compassion with this grapefruit and basil no-alcohol cocktail. Using these complementary ingredients, this recipe helps open hearts to build roads and understanding. Coconut water inspires the serenity of the moon, purifying away old negativity, while fresh grapefruit brings positivity. Topping with nonalcoholic sparkling wine raises intentions to higher matters. With each sip of this happy and soothing cherry and basil spritzer, hearts will open to compassion and true connection. For an alternate version of this recipe, you can use pomelo instead of grapefruit and Thai basil instead of sweet basil.

SERVES 1

2 basil leaves for love and banishing negative energy

2 cherries, pitted for happiness and love

4 drops rose water for love and healing

1 ounce honey for happiness

⅛ teaspoon ground allspice for luck and healing

1 ounce freshly squeezed grapefruit or pomelo juice for positivity

1 ounce coconut water for spirituality and love

½–1 ounce nonalcoholic sparkling white wine (optional)

Large basil leaf, for garnish

1 In your shaker, place the basil for love and affection, smelling its aroma. Add the cherries and rose water for love as well. Add the honey for softening and sprinkle the allspice for healing. Muddle, pounding out any blockages to connection.

2 Add the grapefruit juice and coconut water for spiritual love and purification. Add ice and shake.

3 Strain into a glass and top with nonalcoholic sparkling wine, if using. Garnish with a basil leaf to open the nose (and heart) with each sip.

BEYOND THE GLASS

The aroma of basil can help open the heart and soothe anger, facilitating communication and sympathy. As a garnish, it sets the tone for the compassionate energy of this mocktail before even sipping. But also the shape of basil is naturally curved, creating a little boat when flipped upside down. This offers the opportunity to add not just other aromatics but also a little magic by using it as a metaphorical "boat" to symbolize traveling over calm waters or traversing new lands. Sprinkle other aromatics, such as rose water or dried rose petals, in the boat shape to create a magical aroma upon each sip and infuse with the intention of open hearts taking your connection beyond troubled waters.

AFFIRMATIONS TO SIP BY:
Each sip stokes my inner fire.
Energy combines; new ideas are inspired.
Every fiber of my being is beaming with passion.

PASSIONFIRE

Passion, Creativity, Love

Light up the night with this fiery pomegranate and cayenne elixir. With the creative energy of pomegranate-based grenadine, orange, and spicy fresh red pepper for fidelity and heated love, this is just the mocktail to inspire your inner fire—whether for creativity or lust. Layered with burgundy grenadine on the bottom, orange in the middle, and a red hibiscus float on top, you symbolically mix energy for passion and creativity through ritually stirring the recipe (turning the drink a fiery autumn hue). Whether looking for a spicy night (and drink) to share with your partner or seeking to inspire exciting ideas for a passion project, this is just the sip to stoke your inner fire.

SERVES 1

Ground cayenne and salt or sugar, for rim

¼ ounce Grenadine (page 199 in the appendix)

2–3 slices fresh chile pepper for passion

1 ounce passionfruit juice for love

1½ ounces freshly squeezed orange juice for love and luck

½ ounce Hibiscus Tea (page 199 in the appendix) for lust and love

Orange peel and cinnamon stick, for garnish

1 Prepare a glass with a cayenne and salt or sugar rim—a circle of spice to encircle you and your beloved.

2 In the bottom of your glass(es), place the grenadine. Pomegranate has plentiful seeds and so carries the symbolism of fertility and abundance. Add the chile pepper and muddle thoroughly to integrate the spice.

3 Add ice and, using the back of a spoon to add it slowly, layer the passionfruit juice and then the orange juice. Then, layer the tea on top.

4 Garnish with an orange twist (see "Beyond the Glass" below for an added trick) and, using a cinnamon stick, stir the drink while saying any affirmation that matches the mood while mixing the ingredients together.

BEYOND THE GLASS

The oils in citrus peels are what make it such a powerful garnish in mixology, but they are also oils that can catch fire. When done safely, it makes the perfect magical addition to fan the flames of your fire in this potion. To experiment, peel a piece of citrus. Lightly hold the peel with the rind facing your drink, then squeeze it. Notice the citrus oils squirt out as you look closely. When doing this over a flame, you will get a burst of fire. To do so, take a fresh peel of orange and being careful not to bend it, hold it slightly above a match, allowing the oils to warm. Without letting your fingers burn, quickly squeeze the peel with intention and watch the flames roar like those of your inner fire.

AFFIRMATIONS TO SIP BY:

Each sip opens hearts.

I embrace a deeper, fulfilling romance.

Love overflows my cup.

ROSE AND MAPLE FROZEN DAIQUIRI

Love, Sensuality, Connection

Deepen your connection with this red wine and rose frozen nonalcoholic daiquiri. Sweetened with maple for grounding and longevity in love and lightly spiced with cardamom, this is just the decadent elixir for a romantic evening or tuning into your sensuality. With its enchanting pink color and unique ingredient incorporation, this is an easy and addicting recipe you and your partner will enjoy. This drink is a perfect example of how with just a touch of creativity and magic you can enjoy those cocktail classics without the alcohol. Enjoy on your own for a bit of healthy, feel-good indulgence or share with a partner for a love potion.

½ ounce maple syrup for love and longevity

Pinch of ground cardamom for love and sensuality

1 ounce freshly squeezed lime juice for healing and love

4 drops orange bitters (optional) for love and luck

¼ ounce nonalcoholic red wine (optional) for sensuality

Rose Tea (page 200 in the appendix) ice cubes for love and healing

Sprinkle of rose petals and cardamom, for garnish

1. In advance, freeze rose tea into ice cubes. If making recipe on the fly, you can add 1 ounce of rose tea directly to your shaker. Then shake, and strain the recipe with ice.
2. In a blender, place the maple syrup and sprinkle the cardamom for love. Add the lime juice, bitters, and red wine. Add the tea ice cubes (start with 3; add more as needed) and blend.
3. Strain into a daiquiri glass and garnish, saying any affirmations that resonate as you fill your cup.

BEYOND THE GLASS

Garnet's deep burgundy color doesn't just match the color of the red wine in this recipe but also is a stone of passion and sensuality. It can be just the stone to inspire deep connection and romance. Add the stone as a centerpiece between you and your partner while sipping, or hold if drinking alone, to inspire passion.

AFFIRMATIONS TO SIP BY:
Sunshine radiates in my heart.
I release woe and worries.
I embrace the joy of the moment.

SUMMER SUN SIPPER

Love, Happiness, Joy

Nothing is quite as bright and energizing as the summertime sun. Inspire a bit of that radiance and excitement at your gathering with this Summer Sun raspberry, basil, and pineapple mocktail. Pineapple promotes hospitality, while basil banishes negative energy and opens the heart. With the way paved, raspberry, orange, and lemon bring some happiness and liquid sunshine! This bright, yummy elixir will help inspire some radiance at your gathering. Or enjoy on your own to relax and connect with joy.

SERVES 1

1 ounce honey for happiness

6–8 raspberries for happiness and love

2–3 leaves basil for affection and banishing negative energy

1 ounce freshly squeezed orange juice for joy

1 ounce pineapple for hospitality

1 ounce freshly squeezed lemon juice

Pineapple leaf, raspberries, and a pineapple slice, for garnish

1. In a glass, place the honey to soothe, as well as the raspberries and basil. Muddle the fresh ingredients, then add ice, orange juice, pineapple, and lemon juice.

2. Stir. Garnish and say an affirmation while sipping, allowing sunshine to seep into your heart.

BEYOND THE GLASS

Orange calcite is a solar stone that invites playfulness and creativity. It can also inspire confidence, which is perfect for letting one feel vibrant and safe to connect. While sipping this concoction, hold the calcite stone at your stomach, feeling the resonance between the orange juice and the crystal. Keeping it on your person at a gathering can help you channel some of that warm solar energy to authentic connection.

AFFIRMATIONS TO SIP BY:

I embrace and celebrate my feminine energy.

My friendships support and ground me.

My life is full of all kinds of love.

PEACH, MAPLE, AND ROSE BELLINI

Celebration, Feminine Friendship, Fidelity

Celebrate friendship and feminine energy with this fun peach and passionfruit nonalcoholic Bellini. With ingredients for the moon, Venus, and water—the element of emotion—it's a recipe full of feminine energy. Peach, vanilla, and passionfruit create a concoction for love, peace, and passion, while maple inspires longevity of connection. With citrus and a dash of rose water for floral energy and love, this is a great recipe whether you want to embrace your feminine side or celebrate the women in your life.

SERVES 1

3 slices peach for love, happiness, and feminine wisdom

½ ounce maple syrup for love and longevity

¼ teaspoon vanilla extract (optional) for peace

2 ounces passionfruit juice for love and peace

½ ounce freshly squeezed lemon juice for friendship, joy, and longevity

4–8 drops rose water (optional) for feminine love and connection

3 ounces nonalcoholic sparkling white wine

Peach slice and/or rose petals, for garnish

1 In the bottom of a stemless champagne or wine glass, place the peaches—a symbol of wisdom, feminine energy, and love. Drizzle with the maple syrup to ground and keep your connection strong.

2 Muddle the peaches and syrup, then add the vanilla, if using, and the passionfruit juice for peace, the lemon juice for friendship and uplifting, and the rose water, if using, for floral healing and love.

3 Top with sparkling wine and garnish—a drink of celebration, bringing an element of uplifting and excitement.

4 Say any affirmations while clinking glasses.

BEYOND THE GLASS

In the tarot, the Three of Cups depicts three women encircled, holding up glasses in celebration. The card is an indicator of success but also companionship. Oftentimes, our success is the result of teamwork or a supportive system. It takes a village to get us to where we are, after all. So celebrating success and companionship are often intertwined. How can you bring more celebration into your friendships to strengthen bonds and cultivate support?

AFFIRMATIONS TO SIP BY:

With each sip, pretenses fall away.

I release all tension and embrace understanding.

Like bees flowing from flower to flower, we work together in harmony at this hour.

ROSE QUARTZ HARMON-TEA

Healing, Harmony, Psychic Sensitivity

Open hearts like spring flowers with this rose quartz–inspired tea. With rose, lavender, and honey, this mocktail recipe will inspire love and harmony, with its warmth opening the heart with each sip. Make two to share with a guest to inspire calm and peaceful communication or enjoy on your own to connect to universal love and invite yourself to see the beauty in every moment.

SERVES 1

2 teaspoon dried rose petals for love and healing

¼ teaspoon dried lavender for peace and communication

Pinch of ground cardamom for love

3 ounces hot water

1 tablespoon honey for healing, community, and wisdom

½–¾ ounce freshly squeezed lemon juice for friendship and cleansing

1 ounce Lyre's Pink London Spirit (optional)

1. Hold the rose petals in your hand. Envision hearts opening with each sip of this tea, like a rose opening up with an aromatizing scent.
2. In a tea strainer or in the bottom of a tempered cup, add the rose petals and sprinkle in the lavender for calm and communication and the cardamom to warm and open the heart.
3. Pour in the hot water, saying any affirmations now. Cover and let steep for 5 minutes.
4. Stir in the honey for soothing and attractive energy, drawing in your desired outcome like bees to a flower.
5. Add the lemon juice for cleansing the past and for joy and friendship, as well as the nonalcoholic substitute, if using.
6. For a chilled version, let cool or add ice for a tea-based cold, refreshing mocktail. This recipe also makes a great option for tasseography (see chapter 8).

BEYOND THE GLASS

Rose quartz, the namesake of this drink, connects you with universal love. Associated with the heart, this pink-hued crystal can help soften hearts and invite gratefulness. Adding a piece to your coffee table, wherever you plan to sit, or even holding it in your hand can help soften the energy and invite peaceful, loving energy. Thinking of your intention (and prior to any guests' arrival), hold the stone to your heart. Envision a rose opening up. Place the stone somewhere where its energy will infuse into the area, or keep it on your person to inspire peaceful, loving connection to the universe.

AFFIRMATIONS TO SIP BY:
I embrace harmony in every connection.
Peace and ease inspire clear communication and authenticity.
Joy overflows in every cup.

HIBISCUS-LAVENDER ICED TEA

Love, Positivity, Peace

Lower blood pressure and bring peace and joy with this three- to five-ingredient hibiscus-lavender elixir. This tea is one of my fast and easy go-tos for a fun and lovely gathering. With as little as three ingredients, it can be ready in minutes and batched to serve multiple people at once. Be careful, though—it's often gone in a flash. With the fun and sensuality of hibiscus, the calming of lavender, and a little bit of sweetness, it's perfect for giving your gathering a lively, communicative edge. For sweetness and citrus, you can add agave or your choice of sweetener as well as grapefruit for some positivity.

SERVES 5 OR 6

4 tablespoons dried hibiscus
for lust and love

1 tablespoon dried lavender
for peace and communication

4 cups boiling water

3 ounces agave (optional)
for love and youth

3 ounces freshly squeezed grapefruit juice (optional)
for purification and positivity

Lavender sprig, for garnish

1. In a French press or a large strainer set over a mug, place the hibiscus and lavender. Hover your hands above these herbs, reflecting on their ability to lighten the mood. Say any affirmations that resonate, then pour in the water.

2. Let steep for 5 minutes, until a deep, dark magenta or burgundy. Add the agave and/or grapefruit juice, if using.

3. Pour over ice into your glass and garnish with a fresh lavender sprig for a floral element to enhance each sip with relaxation and peace.

BEYOND THE GLASS

Hibiscus has a tropical essence that easily inspires joy. Magically, it is used for lust and love and to aid divination. Its antioxidants help reinforce the body against inflammation and oxidative stress, and it can help lower blood pressure and improve blood sugar regulation. Combined here with lavender and grapefruit, it helps to inspire joy and zest by bringing deep ease. By relaxing, we can allow more happiness, joy, and love into our lives and connect on a more authentic level. How can you invite more relaxation to allow fun and connection to flow with ease in your life?

AFFIRMATIONS TO SIP BY:
I embrace the joyful spirits of spring and nature.
Nature revitalizes my spirit.
I appreciate the beauty of nature.

FAIRY FUN MOCKTAIL

Fairies, Happiness, Love

Increase your awareness of other realms and entice your energy (and taste buds) with this ethereal, zesty lavender and blackberry fae-inspired spritzer. It's a great choice when looking to connect to the excitable energy of nature or enhance an outdoor meeting with friends with a fun elixir. Thyme adds themes of growth, love, and psychic awareness, providing a gorgeous leaflike garnish. Blackberry brings excitable fairy energy, lust, luck, and healing, while lavender inspires peace and happiness. Finished with the exciting effect of color-changing butterfly pea flower, it easily inspires joy and is perfect for summer solstice or midsummer celebrations.

SERVES 1

2–4 blackberries, plus an extra, for garnish for fairies and luck

2 sprigs thyme, plus an extra, for garnish for love and healing

1 ounce Honey Syrup (page 199 in the appendix) for happiness

½ ounce freshly squeezed lime juice

3 drops of nonalcoholic lavender bitters (such as All The Bitter) (optional) for fairies and peace

1 ounce soda water

½–1 ounce Butterfly Pea Flower Tea (page 200 in appendix) for youth, happiness, and transformation

1. In your glass, place the blackberries and two thyme sprigs. Add the syrup and muddle, thinking of muddling down your worries and living in the moment with the movement.
2. Add the lime juice to cleanse anything that limits your excitement and then add the bitters, if using, for peace.
3. Add ice and the soda water. Then layer the flower tea on top, which adds a deep blue-purple hue for transformation.
4. Garnish with the remaining thyme sprig for evergreen growth. Say any affirmations as you sip, feeling the supportive energy of the drink inspire joy and excitement.

BEYOND THE GLASS

Great for tranquility, lavender is excellent for promoting the mind for intuition and psychic sight. A known relaxant, this flower helps purify energy to inspire peace and happiness, allowing one's inspiration and ideas to flow through easily. Plus, its association with the fae makes it perfect for the magic of this recipe! Allow the magic of this floral ingredient to uplift your senses and inspire freedom with each sip. You can even soften your gaze while looking at plant life and invite yourself to see their energy.

The MAGIC of GARNISHES

When used correctly, garnishes are an act of magic—they curate aromas with which to allure before even taking the first sip. The right garnish can create layers of sophistication, a symphony between the aromas on the nose and the flavors in the drink. One of my most favorite garnishes was a citrus peel "boat" floating atop the drink holding dried jasmine flowers and rose petals within its curl. The scent of the jasmine, rose, and lemon aroma added layers of attracting floral essences, a contrast to the earthy way those ingredients expressed themselves in the body of the drink. Adding a garnish intentionally to influence the experience and energy of your drink can set the stage for a supremely magical mocktail, especially when sharing with another. Here are a few common garnishes and how, when used intentionally, they can enhance connection.

MINT: A sprig of mint can refresh and renew the mind with each sip, helping to clear your thoughts and invite calm. For a mint sprig garnish, you will want to stimulate its oils by slapping it against the back of or between your hands.

BASIL: Basil can add a slightly sweet, peppery, or spicy herbaceous aroma. It can be protective and dispels negativity, but it also helps open the heart. Like mint, basil also needs to be stimulated by slapping it between your hands. A slapped basil leaf can also float atop the drink for a gentle garnish.

ROSEMARY: Like the cleansing sea breeze for which is its named (see the Clear Mind Mint Julep in chapter 5), rosemary makes a great garnish to bring peace and cleanse the mind. It can also be smoked for cleansing, clarity, and remembrance.

CULINARY SAGE: A sage garnish can facilitate purification and wisdom. It brings an earthy, woodsier aroma and like rosemary can also be torched for cleansing smoke to clear energy before even taking the first sip.

CINNAMON STICK: Cinnamon is a manifestative ingredient, and using it as a garnish also offers the opportunity to stir your drink with intention. It can also be lightly flamed for a smoky cinnamon aroma and incense in one.

FRESH OR DRIED EDIBLE FLOWERS: Edible flowers can bring a fragrant aroma that cannot be replicated even when adding the same floral ingredient through syrup or bitters. As a garnish, they can create depth and entice through smell. Using a rose water or orange blossom/flower water spritz, you can simulate this effect.

CITRUS WHEELS: You'll often see dehydrated citrus wheels as garnishes. Using a wheel, you can drop a few bitters atop it for a dynamic aroma.

CITRUS PEELS: If you look closely at the skin of citrus, you'll see it has little pores. Inside each one is citrus oil. Expressing (by squeezing) a citrus peel over a drink is a common garnish that adds the oils of the citrus. You can also smoke a peel or express it over a flame for fiery energy and to add citrus smoke essence to a drink. Citrus peels are usually twisted after expression and balanced on the edge of a glass, but they also can be used as a "boat" upon which you can float other garnishes, like dried teas, flowers, or even bitters. Here are the specific energies of each citrus (or you can refer to the citrus section in chapter 3 for more nuanced descriptions).

- **Lime**—love, healing, hex-breaking, protection.
- **Lemon**—uplifting, friendship, cleansing, the moon.
- **Orange**—joy, happiness, wellness, awakening.
- **Grapefruit**—purification, positivity.

CHAPTER 7

WELL-BEING AND WELLNESS

Potions for Self-Care, Healing, and Vitality

Whether it's curling up with a hot tea to fight an oncoming cold or drinking a revitalizing morning smoothie, what we sip not only nurtures our body with beneficial ingredients but can also boost our mood and energy. The recipes in this chapter will help you utilize what you put into your body for holistic wellness—nonalcoholic potions for self-care, healing, beauty, and vitality. Inspire peaceful, deep rest with the chamomile, cherry, and rosemary Restful Witch or cultivate your inner and outer glow with the Pineapple-Turmeric Glow Elixir.

Since part of wellness is also self-care, this can include meditations or rituals, such as the Flower Moon Mocktail and corresponding tea bath or the Peach and Sage Longevi-tea accompanied with a meditation on trees and the integrated nature of the body. To boost your self-care potential, you'll also uncover how to make healing tea baths and other wellness potions such as bath salts, scrubs, and face masks that correspond to your drinks. This way, your potions can become the ultimate vehicle for self-care rituals and create energetic resonance between what you put both in and on your body.

The mind, body, and spirit connection highlights how the various parts of us influence each other. Through supporting our physical body by being conscious about what we ingest, we can boost our mood and our sense of vitality, and inspire total well-being.

AFFIRMATIONS TO SIP BY:

I am grounded and stable.

My roots grow deep, nourishing me with Mother Earth's supportive energy.

My mind, like branches outstretched to the wide sky, is receptive to divine wisdom.

PEACH AND SAGE LONGEVI-TEA

Purification, Wisdom, Longevity

Tea is a pastime of connecting to the sacred energy within our spiritual and physical cups. Inspired by the ritual and discovery of tea, this peach and sage tea mocktail is a meditative sip for longevity and wisdom. Maple adds the rooted, grounded energy of trees, while green tea and sage awaken your conscious mind to new and expansive thoughts—like branches outstretched to the sky. Complemented by fruity flavors of peach—symbolic of the fruit born from enduring trees—this is a drink for purification, wisdom, and longevity. You can also use plum or other stone fruit instead of peach, if peach is out of season.

SERVES 1

4 peach slices for longevity and blessings

5 sage leaves for longevity and wisdom

¾ ounce maple syrup for longevity and grounded roots

1 ounce freshly squeezed lemon juice for uplifting

3 ounces Green Tea (page 199 in the appendix) for the conscious mind

2 fresh sage leaves, for garnish

1. In the bottom of a glass, place the peach for longevity and the sage for wisdom.
2. Add the maple syrup for grounded tree roots and muddle while saying any affirmation that resonates with you currently.
3. Balance the sweetness with uplifting lemon juice and then add ice, pour in the tea, stir to mix, and garnish.

BEYOND THE GLASS

Like a tree, you are an integrated system in which each part is essential for successful living: being rooted to absorb nutrients, a strong trunk to bear the storm, and leaves to absorb the sunlight and provide shade to contribute to the ecosystem. How can you equally nurture such parts of yourself to bear the fruits of success you seek?

AFFIRMATIONS TO SIP BY:

I am calm and engaged.

Harmony and peaceful vitality fill my being.

I embrace the abundant, restorative energy of the universe.

STRAWBERRY FIELDS

Energy, Love, Harmony

Bring harmony and happiness while energizing your mind with this strawberry and matcha latte. Sometimes we need a midday caffeine kick. Rather than something bitter or loaded with caffeine, though, you can uplift your energy and your mood. With fresh strawberries muddled into milk, you have a pink base to this recipe, topped with green matcha. Harmonized with lavender for peace, this Strawberry Fields recipe is designed both to give you energy and to inspire a smile.

SERVES 1

1 teaspoon matcha powder for harmony and vitality

½ ounce hot water

3 strawberries for love and harmony

2 ounces Lavender-Agave Syrup (page 199 in the appendix) or 1 ounce agave

¼ teaspoon sakura blossom power (optional)

3 ounces milk (such as almond)

1 ounce heavy cream

1 Stir matcha powder with hot (but not boiling) water and set aside to cool.

2 In your shaker, place the strawberries. Add the syrup for peace, then muddle to mix with the strawberries. As you do, envision stamping away anything that brings down your inner peace and harmony. Sprinkle in optional sakura blossom powder, if desired.

3 Add the dairy and ice and shake. Pour into a tall glass, then add more ice. Layer the cooled matcha—a green color of growth atop the harmonizing, loving pink—while saying any affirmations that appeal. Stir to mix ingredients.

BEYOND THE GLASS

When we refuel our bodies with caffeine, it can often overstimulate or cause stress or the jitters. But energizing your body *can* be a harmonious and happy experience. This drink is named for both the ingredients and the visuals of this recipe: the white, red, and green of abundant floral strawberry fields. But it's also about the energy behind these ingredients—the happy, harmonious energy of strawberries, nurturing milk, and revitalizing matcha. Matcha is the tea most commonly used in the harmonious and tranquil Japanese tea ceremonies, providing a more natural, serene energy boost for focus. As you sip this drink, reflect on the properties of the tea and the joyful energy of strawberries and their abundant fields. How can you nurture your body with revitalizing energy that gives way to harmony and abundance? Or, conversely, how can bringing more tranquility invite happiness and natural vitality?

AFFIRMATIONS TO SIP BY:

With each exhale, I release all my worries.

My body and mind are at ease.

Intentional rest resets, rejuvenates, and restores my being.

RESTFUL WITCH

Peace of Mind, Rejuvenation, Rest

The Sleepy Girl Mocktail took the online world by storm. This cherry and magnesium concoction awoke the world to the fact that mocktails can be beneficial, tasty, *and* aesthetically pleasing. In Restful Witch, the benefits of tart cherry and magnesium are bolstered with magical ingredients for peace: chamomile for rest and relaxation and rosemary for peace of mind. The drink uses optional yuzu juice for an enticing citrus note that isn't as acidic as lemon, while adding some awakening magic. This is a peaceful, balanced mocktail with sleep and rest-oriented ingredients that will bring a cooling essence as you sip—perfect for relaxation and calm whether before bed or unwinding after a long day. In place of the lavender-agave syrup, you can use ¼ ounce agave or simple syrup.

SERVES 1

1 ounce Chamomile Tea (page 199 in the appendix) for sleep

Magnesium powder (optional)

1 ounce tart cherry juice

½ ounce Lavender-Agave Syrup (page 199 in the appendix) for peace

½ ounce freshly squeezed yuzu juice or ¾ ounce freshly squeezed lemon juice for rejuvenation

1 ounce soda water

Rosemary sprig, for garnish

1. In a glass, place the tea and, if desired, magnesium powder.
2. Add the cherry juice, the Lavender-Agave Syrup for clearing the mind, and the yuzu for winter rejuvenation or lemon.
3. Add ice and top with the soda water. Garnish with a rosemary sprig, using it to stir the concoction while saying aloud any affirmation that appeals to you currently.

BEYOND THE GLASS

In chapter 4, you learned how making a mocktail can be a ritual itself, and you learned about aligning your breath to the recipe-making process for more relaxation. You can also harmonize your breath with each sip. The 4-7-8 breathing pattern has been shown to aid in relaxation when stressed: breathe in for four seconds, hold for seven, and exhale for eight. Accompany your sipping experience with this breathing exercise, envisioning breathing out any worries and inviting your body to release tension with each exhale.

AFFIRMATIONS TO SIP BY:
I connect in gratitude to the earth.
The moon and earth support and nourish me.
I find calm, restorative energy within.

YERBA MATÉ LATTE

Energy, Nurturing, Earth Connection

This Yerba Maté Latte is just the warming drink you need to put a pep in your step and start your day with the warm embrace of the earth. For many Westerners, starting the day with a hot cup of coffee is an irreplaceable ritual. But that acidic drink can also contribute to dental decay and acid reflux and lead to the drink being less effective over time. For me, a yerba maté latte was the solution—it supplied the warmth and nurturing energy to wake me up but also contained the energy of connection and gratitude to the earth. What better way to start the day? With maple for tree roots, milk to connect to the moon, and allspice for healing, this Yerba Maté Latte is a great way to start the day with an intentional drink and gratitude ritual or share with another to inspire health and connection.

SERVES 1

8 ounces (1 cup) water

1 tablespoon yerba maté for earth and connection

1 tablespoon cold water

1–1½ tablespoon maple syrup for earth magic and longevity

4 tablespoons almond or coconut milk for nurturing and the moon

¼ teaspoon ground allspice

1 Set the water to warm, but don't allow it to boil all the way. Meanwhile, place the yerba maté in the bottom of your cup or in a tea strainer. Wet it with cold water to prevent burning.

2 Once the water is very warm but not boiling, add it to the tea and steep for 5–7 minutes.

3 Meanwhile, in a separate container, combine the maple syrup with the milk—almond for earth connection and prosperity or coconut for the nurturing moon. Warm the milk and maple mixture and, if available, use a frothing wand to produce a nice airy texture, like the clouds of the yerba maté origin myth.

4 In your desired mug, strain out the yerba maté. Then add the allspice, top with the milk, and stir. As you enjoy each sip, reflect in gratitude with the earth.

BEYOND THE GLASS

In chapter 1, you learned about yerba maté and how it is used to connect community. In one of its legends, this plant was believed to be a gift from the moon and clouds. Reflect on the cream in your drink akin to the moon or clouds and the base herb as the earth. As you sip, connect to these stories—how through the nurturing of the earth and moon, abundance comes to manifest and how nourishing your connections can bring health and vitality. Give gratitude for your connection to the earth.

AFFIRMATIONS TO SIP BY:
I am worthy.
I appreciate my body for supporting how far I've come.
I radiate love, compassion, and appreciation for how my experiences have shaped me.

SELF-LOVE PAPAYA POTION

Beauty, Love, Self-Care

Sip in some self-love with papaya, grapefruit, and rose honey. With health-conscious ingredients that are soothing to the body, this Self-Love Papaya Potion is a guilt-free addition to your self-care night rituals. Papaya is loaded with essential digestive enzymes and invites love, beauty, and feminine energy. With a rose-honey syrup that is ready in minutes, you have a gentle sweetener (without adding too much sugar) that supports health, happiness, and spirituality, bolstered by the loving and healing energy of rose. And, of course, what is a feel-good drink without a bit of bubbly? Peaceful, lightly floral, and with a gentle tartness, this embodied elixir will uplift your energy and inspire appreciation for your inner and outer beauty, whether it's soaking in a rose bath or a day with friends.

SERVES 1

2 slices papaya for feminine energy, beauty, and love

1 ounce Rose-Honey Syrup (page 199 in the appendix) for love

2 ounces freshly squeezed grapefruit juice for uplifting

4 drops nonalcoholic lavender bitters (such as All The Bitter) (optional) for inner peace and relaxation

3 ounces nonalcoholic sparkling white wine

Papaya slice and rosebud, for garnish

1 In the bottom of a glass, place the papaya and drizzle the alluring, loving rose-honey syrup.

2 Muddle the papaya and syrup while saying any affirmation that appeals to you. Think on the meaning of the ingredients as you do so.

3 Add the grapefruit juice to boost your mood and a few drops of bitters for relaxation and inner peace.

4 Add ice and top with the sparkling wine. Garnish with a papaya slice that showcases the inner sun/star inside the fruit, to remind you of your inner star power (and for a nice, tasty treat).

BEYOND THE GLASS

The Star card of the tarot depicts a naked woman pouring out two vessels, one onto earth and one onto land. In mysticism, the element of earth symbolizes the physical, while water is the realm of feeling. Through pouring nourishing liquid into both elements on the card, the land flourishes. It is a reminder of the importance of nourishing our emotions, spirit, and body to bring about the best for ourselves. What are some things—no matter how small or trivial—that nourish your body and your spirit? How can you incorporate these into your life more?

AFFIRMATIONS TO SIP BY:
My beauty shines within and around me.
I attract my desires like bees to a flower.
I blossom in my own time.

FLOWER MOON MOCKTAIL

Peace, Beauty, Healing

Whether you're celebrating the flower moon or the abundance and beauty of spring, this mocktail is a great way to sip in the energy and magic of flowers! A rose and calendula relaxing elixir, this recipe uses the energy of flowers to soften your heart, see your inner beauty, and aid it in shining brighter. While each type of flower can have a more nuanced energy and meaning, they are generally symbols of love, beauty, joy, and abundance. Flowers bloom in their own time, reminding us of the importance of care and nurturing. Further, their vibrant colors and aromas attract bees to help pollinate, the same way that inner beauty and kindness can attract love and support. Using a blend of flowers (or, alternatively, just rose), attracting honey, heart-opening basil and cardamom, and uplifting lemon, this refreshing tea mocktail is a perfect sip for some flower magic.

SERVES 1

½–2 teaspoons dried rose petals, plus an extra pinch, for garnish for love

½ teaspoon dried violet (optional)

1 teaspoon calendula (optional) for luck

3 ounces hot water

2–3 teaspoons honey for alluring

3 basil leaves, separated

⅛ teaspoon cardamom for love

¾ ounce freshly squeezed lemon juice

1. Place the rose petals (and violet and calendula, if using) in a tempered/heat-safe cup. If not using the violet and calendula, use 2 teaspoons rose petals.
2. Add the hot water and let steep for 5–7 minutes (a proper steep will allow for the pink color).
3. After 5–7 minutes, add the honey and stir it in until dissolved.
4. Add 2 basil leaves and sprinkle in cardamom for love and comfort.
5. Add the lemon and ice, then shake and strain into stemmed and chilled glassware.
6. Garnish with the extra basil leaf and/or rose petals.

BEYOND THE GLASS

The rose is often a symbol for attraction and love (and its color can denote further meanings). While accompanied with thorns, it also comes with built-in boundaries for protection. When we attract, it is also important to be discerning. Thus, the symbolism of the rose is perfect for a protective attraction visualization—to bring in good energy and deflect the bad. As you sip this floral rose recipe, envision yourself surrounded by a rose bush. What do the roses attract while the thorns keep negativity away?

FLOWER MOON TEA AURA BATH

Turning a Mocktail into a Bath Time Ritual

When your inner beauty shines brightly and you are tuned in to your worth and sense of self-confidence, it can enhance your aura with a glow to help attract blessings. Give your aura a boost with this simple bath time ritual.

Just like making tea, you can infuse a mixture of water with safe herbal ingredients and add them to your bath to infuse your skin and energy with their benefits. This can be an effortless way to turn your drink experience into a full tea bath ritual by using the same or similar ingredients used in your tea-based mocktail. Not only is this simple and easy to prepare while you make your tea for the drink anyway but also it's a supremely magical way to relax.

By using the same ingredients in the Flower Moon Mocktail recipe in this bath time ritual, you can create a resonance between the energy within and the energy without. While this ritual is crafted specifically with the Flower Moon Mocktail in mind, you can use this as a bouncing-off point and change the ingredients to match whatever tea mocktail you choose to make. Just be sure to always check for skin and digestive safety.

2 cups hot water

½ tablespoon dried lavender

1 tablespoon dried rose petals

½ tablespoon dried basil for affection

1 tablespoon dried calendula for luck

Flower Moon Mocktail

1 Set your bathtub to fill with water while you prepare this mixture.

2 In a small pot, bring the water to a boil.

3 Bring it to a low simmer and add the dried ingredients.

4 Stir the pot clockwise, thinking on your spiritual radiance drawing in your desires effortlessly, or even just good energy and positive vibes.

5 After 15 minutes, take the pot off the heat and add it to the bath filled with water. Strain the herbs/flowers to avoid a pipe clog if that is something you are worried about. Alternatively, you can add the herbs to a muslin bag and add straight to the bath instead of boiling.

6 With your drink in hand, slip in to the bath. Think on the floral ingredients you are ingesting and the resonance of the same ingredients surrounding you in the bath, infusing your energy and aura.

AFFIRMATIONS TO SIP BY:

The moon soothes my spirit.

Healing flows with ease into my life.

Peace is my birthright.

MELON MOON COOLER

Spirituality, Healing, Inner Peace

When it comes to tea in mocktails, you run the danger of it being too watery. Luckily, watermelon has just enough water not to need any extra ice for this cooling jasmine and coconut healing elixir. Jasmine green tea brings peace and spirituality to the mind, and coconut water invites psychic awareness. Five ingredients and just a little prep work and you have a hydrating, low-acid recipe for healing and spirituality. Instead of blending, you can alternatively muddle fresh watermelon and shake with ice.

SERVES 1

Himalayan salt, for rim (optional)

1 cup frozen watermelon
for healing

2 ounces chilled Jasmine Green Tea (page 200 in the appendix)
for spirituality and peace of mind

1 ounce coconut water
for spirituality

½ ounce agave, plus more to taste

1 ounce Lyre's White Cane Spirit or Agave Blanco (optional)

1 Rim your glass with Himalayan salt for healing, if using.

2 In a blender, place the watermelon and pour in the tea and coconut water for soothing.

3 Add the agave to taste, any nonalcoholic optional spirits, and blend.

4 Pour into a small glass and enjoy, feeling the cooling essence of the healing ingredients. Say any affirmations that resonate now.

BEYOND THE GLASS

Coconut water is harvested from young green coconuts and in magic is associated with the moon. And since it is 94% water, it helps hydrate the body while being low in sugar and calories. Spiritually, coconut is used to connect to the moon, bring internal purification, and increase love or spiritual and psychic awareness. It is also a great way to increase the volume of your mocktail recipes! While sipping, reflect on the nurturing, supportive qualities of the ingredients replenishing your body and senses.

AFFIRMATIONS *to* SIP BY:

I glow from the inside out.

I celebrate my inner and outer beauty.

I am a radiant, vibrant being.

PINEAPPLE-TURMERIC GLOW ELIXIR

Radiance, Happiness, Purification

What you ingest impacts not only your mood but also your skin. Cultivate your inner and outer glow with pineapple, kiwi, and coconut milk. Pineapple is a vibrant fruit associated with love, healing, and hospitality, and it can also help with aging skin. Creamy coconut milk with rose honey makes for an alluring sip, inspiring both beauty and hydration. Fresh turmeric and pineapple fuel joy—a warmth that will radiate from the inside out. You can even pair the recipe with a homemade face mask for rejuvenation.

SERVES 1

3 slices kiwi, plus an extra, for garnish

1 ounce Rose-Honey or Honey Syrup (page 199 in the appendix) for love and beauty

1 ounce pineapple juice for healing, love, and joy

¼ teaspoon ground turmeric

1 ounce coconut milk for inner purification

1 ounce Green Tea (page 199 in the appendix)

½ ounce freshly squeezed lemon juice

Pineapple leaf and yellow edible dried flower (like calendula), for garnish

1 In your shaker, place the kiwi. Add the syrup for beauty, the pineapple juice for rejuvenation, and the turmeric for glow. Muddle the kiwi and turmeric into the syrup. Say any affirmations that appeal to you now.

2 Pour in the nurturing, moon-associated coconut milk for soothing and hydration, the tea for its skin benefits, and the lemon juice. Add ice and shake.

3 Strain into a glass over ice and garnish with a pineapple leaf and dried flower, as well as the extra slice of kiwi.

BEYOND THE GLASS

Kiwi is not just a delicious snack; it has more vitamin C than two oranges (great to boost the immune system!) and is a source of vitamins E and K, potassium, and antioxidants in general. Many of its benefits are in its skin, though! So try to purchase organic to confidently eat the peel too. Kiwi is clearly a fruit of health, but it also symbolizes unity, vitality, happiness, and a general openness. Coupled with the other ingredients in this drink, it helps boost your energetic glow. As you sip the recipe and eat the kiwi garnish, reflect on how you can foster more openness to allow your unique radiance to shine through.

SELF-CARE SIPS, RITUALS, AND FACE MASK RECIPES

A true self-care ritual is about well-being and support for mind, body, and spirit so you can keep on keeping on—but in balance with what is going on in your life. What things bring you peace and comfort but are also healthy and supportive? If you're low on funds, what can you do with what you have on hand? If you're low on time or energy, what is something effortless and quick that still nurtures your mental and physical health? It might be taking five minutes for a cup of tea while watching the sunset or taking a quick nourishing bath. In fact, many of the recipes in this book are in themselves an act of self-care.

But even greater resonance awaits. Many of the ingredients in this book can also be used in creating things that nurture the outside, not just the inside. You can create a corresponding face mask, bath salts, or even body scrub to enjoy while you're sipping on your mocktails, fostering energetic resonance between your inner and outer glow, and hopefully curate a ritual for self-care made just for you.

To the right you will find basic recipes to customize your skin-safe drink ingredients into wellness rituals, plus a few specific face mask examples that correspond to drinks already in this book. Alter them to make them your own and make sure to research each ingredient so as not to upset or damage your skin.

Through matching the ingredients in your magical mocktails to these homemade self-care products, you can infuse the energy of your intentions from both the inside and the outside. But this is also a great way to make ingredients go further, such as using papaya for a face mask when you can't possibly eat it all before it goes bad. By doing so, you enhance wellness within and without, turning your mocktail into a magical self-care ritual.

for BATH SALTS

Making bath salts that match your mocktail recipe can be great for cleansing and relaxation, enhancing the enjoyment of the recipe while you sip and soak.

¾ cup salt (such as sea salt or Himalayan salt)

1 cup Epsom salt

¼ cup baking soda

1 tablespoon dried, body-safe herbs

5–10 drops skin-safe essential oils

for SCRUBS

Scrubs can be a great way to combine cleansing, beauty, and protection, especially in situations where you are actively working on cutting cords, or "shedding skin."

½ cup scrub (such as salt, sugar, or coffee grounds)

2–4 teaspoons body-safe oil (such as coconut oil)

5–10 drops skin- and body-safe essential oils

1 teaspoon dried herbs

1 In a glass bowl or jar, mix your scrub base with oil. Add the oil bit by bit, as it can depend on your base scrub and you do not want it to get too watery.

2 Add essential oils and any optional herbs. Depending on the ingredients, you may need to refrigerate it.

for FACE MASKS

Face masks are great to match the magic of your well-being mocktail when working on beauty, radiance, or how you appear to other people. To make a face mask, you need a balance of solid, sticky, and liquid ingredients so that it will stay on your face but also come off.

- **Avocado and coconut (pairs with Earth and Moon Avocado Elixir):** 1 tablespoon avocado + 1 tablespoon honey + ½ tablespoon coconut water + pinch of ground cardamom
- **Pineapple and turmeric (pairs with Pineapple-Turmeric Glow Elixir):** 1 tablespoon muddled fresh pineapple + ¼ teaspoon ground turmeric + 1 teaspoon honey
- **Papaya and rose (pairs with Self-Love Papaya Potion):** ½ cup papaya + ½ teaspoon rose water + 1 tablespoon honey
- **Yogurt and raspberry (pairs with Raspberry Moon Soother):** 1 tablespoon unflavored Greek yogurt + 1 teaspoon honey + 1 raspberry + pinch of ground cinnamon

AFFIRMATIONS TO SIP BY:

My body is in total harmony and health.

I am happy, whole, and balanced.

I support and love my body through its cycles.

RASPBERRY MOON SOOTHER

Happiness, Health, the Moon

Nurture your biome and sweeten your senses with this tangy raspberry and yogurt mocktail. This is a perfect recipe when you want something a little more health conscious, to lift up your spirit and heart. With raspberry for happiness, it has a berry essence to enliven your spirit, while yogurt, coconut water, and honey rebalance your inner biome. This tangy, supportive potion initially started as a recipe to support the monthly feminine cycle, but with its health-conscious ingredients, it's a feel-good sip anytime of the month.

SERVES 1

8 raspberries, plus 2–3 extra, for garnish for happiness

2 tablespoons unflavored nonfat Greek yogurt for the moon

⅛ teaspoon ground cinnamon (optional)

1 ounce Lyre's Italian Orange (optional)

1 ounce Honey Syrup (page 199 in the appendix) for happiness

2 ounces coconut water for the moon

1. In your shaker, place the raspberries, yogurt, optional cinnamon and nonalcoholic spirit, and syrup. You may need to adjust how much syrup you use based on the sweetness of the yogurt.
2. Muddle, then add the coconut water and ice.
3. Shake and strain into a Nick and Nora glass or small stemmed glassware and garnish with a few raspberries for a snack. As you sip, say any affirmation, tuning in to the ingredients.

BEYOND THE GLASS

Named for the moon, moonstone is a powerful stone to connect to goddess energy and enhance one's intuition. It is said to help balance emotions or aid one in connecting to their higher self. It is also a popular stone to work with on one's menstrual cycle. To tune in to the moon for happiness and support with this recipe, hold moonstone as you sip and invite the moon's nurturing light to bring balance and well-being.

AFFIRMATIONS TO SIP BY:

I nourish both spiritual and physical well-being.

With each sip, I awaken my innermost spirit for success.

Every fiber of my being is revitalized.

WINTER WELLNESS

Awakening, Healing, Success

Holiday drinks can often be overloaded with sugar or sweets that make you feel sluggish. Sip on something better for you with this kombucha-spiced apple mocktail. With ginger kombucha to support digestion and added spices like cinnamon, allspice, and nutmeg, plus apple, you don't have to miss out on the seasonal cider. But these warming winter ingredients aren't just about tantalizing flavors; the spices help inspire spiritual energy to raise vibrations and comfort your spirit—perfect for some spiritual awakening amid the cold winter nights.

SERVES 1

¼ ounce freshly squeezed lime juice

2 ounces apple juice for healing and comfort

Pinch of ground cinnamon for success and healing

Pinch of ground allspice

Pinch of ground nutmeg for luck

2 ounces ginger kombucha for awakening

¼ ounce grenadine (page 199 in the appendix)

Rosemary sprig or cinnamon stick, for garnish

1 In your glass, place the lime juice to cleanse, then add the apple juice and sprinkle in the spices.

2 Add ice, then pour in the kombucha, watching the fizz bubble up (as though raising your own energy). Add the grenadine for the magic of pomegranate and watch as it droops down to the bottom of your glass for a layered effect. Stir, garnish, and enjoy.

BEYOND THE GLASS

The winter solstice brings the longest hours of nighttime in a year. It also marks the start of winter. But while the seasonal change may feel dreary for some, the hours of daylight will begin to grow again. So while around this time we often celebrate family and seek warmth, it's also about rebirth—what you might wish to bring into being or nurture within yourself with the growth of the light. Similarly, this recipe both fortifies and comforts. Whether you're celebrating the solstice or echoing those themes in your life at this time, ponder what wants to be reborn within yourself. How can you nourish that intention and bring it to light, like the increase of the sunlight from the winter to summer solstice?

AFFIRMATIONS TO SIP BY:
I radiate an abundance of vitality.
I am motivated to pursue goals aligned with my soul's purpose.
I savor every essence of life's experiences.

SWEET AND SPICY SESAME

Vitality, Courage, Sensuality

Get energy moving with this sweet, spicy, and savory sesame and honey grapefruit spritzer. Life is a mixture of unique and exciting flavors—if you seek them out. Shake up the mundane and experience new things (and flavors) with this revitalizing mocktail. A mixture of savory sesame with pepper and ginger for fiery energy, complemented with almond and grapefruit, this elixir will revitalize and awaken your senses, inspiring vitality. You can use your choice of pomelo or grapefruit and top with white tea for the conscious mind. Instead of nonalcoholic amaretto, you can use white tea and 1/8 teaspoon almond extract.

SERVES 1

2 slices fresh ginger for power

1 ounce Honey Syrup (page 199 in the appendix)

1/8 teaspoon ground red pepper for energy movement

1/8 teaspoon ground cardamom for love

1/8 teaspoon sesame oil for spiritual cleansing and prosperity

2 ounces pomelo or grapefruit juice for purification and positivity

2 ounces nonalcoholic amaretto

Candied or fresh ginger and sesame seeds, for garnish

1 In your shaker, place the ginger for power, as well as the syrup. Muddle to express the ginger's energizing flavor.

2 Sprinkle in the red pepper and cardamom for warming energy, and the sesame oil.

3 Add the pomelo juice, nonalcoholic amaretto, and ice, and shake.

4 Strain into a tall glass over crushed or blended ice, and garnish.

BEYOND THE GLASS

Used in Southeast Asia for over 5,000 years, ginger is a go-to for all kinds of health and vitality matters. A warming root spice, ginger can help promote circulation and the flow of blood, and it is associated with the planet Mars in astrology, as well as the element of fire. In magical folklore, this stimulating root can be used to inspire power and heat things up of all kinds, whether it be success, love, power, money, or even healing and purification. As you sip this recipe, envision ginger energizing your body with your intention.

EARTH AND MOON AVOCADO MOCKTAIL

Nourishment, Fertility, Beauty, Grounding

Nourish your body and your connection to Mother Earth with this avocado, cucumber, and coconut elixir. Between coconut and cucumber for the moon and avocado for the earth, this potion celebrates the abundant capacity of the earth and lunar cycles to nourish our bodies and all life on earth. Besides, it's hard not to feel healthy when drinking avocado—as a great source of healthy fats, omega 3, and vitamins C, E, K, and B6, it can also help stabilize blood sugar and help you feel fuller.[10] By drinking it with hydrating coconut water, you are fueling your body with some good stuff! When mixed with cucumber, refreshing mint, and even rose for beauty, this healthy, earthy elixir helps hydrate the body with beneficial ingredients that contribute to an inner and outer glow. I can't imagine a more savory way to attune to the abundant blessings of the earth and moon and do something nourishing for both body and beauty!

AFFIRMATIONS TO SIP BY:

I nourish, love, and appreciate my body.

I am connected to Mother Earth and Moon and grateful for all the abundance they nurture in my life.

Each and every day, I grow with gratitude.

recipe continued on page 130

SERVES 1

Sea salt, for rim

4 slices cucumber, plus an extra, for garnish for lunar beauty, peace, and healing

¼ cup avocado for beauty and love

7 leaves mint, plus an extra sprig, for garnish for calm and refreshment

⅛ teaspoon of ground cardamom for love

3 ounces coconut water for spirituality and love

1 ounce freshly squeezed lime juice for healing and cleansing

1 ounce agave

1 Begin by rimming your glass with salt, for connecting to the grounding and restorative nature of Mother Earth and the Moon-ruled ocean.

2 In your shaker, place the cucumber for lunar beauty and fertility, the avocado for loving earth energy, and the mint to rejuvenate your senses. Muddle these while thinking of the fertile energy of the earth and lunar cycles. Say any affirmations that appeal to you now, using the kinetic energy of the movement to infuse your intention into the drink.

3 Sprinkle in cardamom for love and add the coconut water for hydrating lunar energy, with which to nourish both your body and intentions.

4 Add the lime juice for cleansing, reflecting on what you are freeing your energy from.

5 Then add the agave and ice. Shake hard to integrate flavors, then strain or pour into your finished glass over ice.

6 Garnish with a mint sprig and and/or cucumber slice. As you sip, visualize your body breaking down the beverage and the energy of the moon and earth spreading nourishing energy to every fiber of your being.

BEYOND THE GLASS

From ancient farmers watching the moon for weather patterns to folklore on when to plant or prune based on the phase of the lunar cycle, the moon and earth have always had a dance of fertility and abundance. The moon's phases are a result of its orientation in relation to the earth and sun, and in lunar gardening, these varying phases are seen to influence the growth of plants: The waxing cycle is a time to nourish a plant's aboveground growth, while the waning cycle is for pruning and cutting back. And it holds an important lesson: knowing when to plant, nourish, harvest, and cut back and how our emotional and spiritual state—our inner moon—can nourish or hinder that. What phase are you in—is it time to grow, ground, release, or restore? What intention are you nourishing your body with?

CHAPTER 8

INSIGHT

Ritualistic Sips for Reflection, Hope, and Wisdom

Meditating over a cup of tea has been a sacred pastime for centuries. However, your spiritual sips don't have to be limited to this hot beverage—diverse beverages for spiritual wisdom await you. Foster perseverance by connecting to the lessons of the desert through the smoky Desert Blossom with dragon fruit, sage, and agave. Perhaps cultivate inner peace and mindfulness for the moment with the cucumber and jasmine green tea Jasmine Peace Potion.

What we drink carries the potential to expand our minds to something greater. From connecting to spirit for hope and insight or lifting the mind for clarity, these sips help you cultivate inner wisdom and deep understanding. Many are infused with reflection and meditations to glean insight in times of transition and change, and since the moon is the core of many mindful and spiritual rituals, there are recipes to channel its power.

What you sip can help prompt reflection, inspire mindfulness, and even bring spiritual insight. Uncover how to add ritual and spirituality to your drinks, such as incorporating a tea leaf reading to turn your spiritual sips into a divinatory method for insight or unravel the symbolism of your chalice through the tarot. Your mocktail recipes can inspire hope, trust, and calm. And in turn, you will cultivate a sense of trust in something greater.

AFFIRMATIONS TO SIP BY:
My mind is present in the moment.
I appreciate the here and now.
I savor the essence of every moment, for they can never be recaptured again.

JASMINE PEACE POTION

Tranquility, Spirituality, Mindfulness

Create inner peace by tuning in to the present moment with this cucumber, jasmine, and lavender mocktail. Each sip of this potion is an invitation to experience mindfulness—from fresh cucumber and lemon to rejuvenate, to rosemary and lavender for cleansing and relaxation. Lightly sweetened with honey, the centerpiece of this potion is jasmine green tea—invoking the spiritual, peaceful energies of jasmine and the conscious mind elements of green tea. Together, it is a light and insightful recipe that encourages relaxation and meditation. Enjoy while watching the wildlife around you to unwind and connect to nature after a long day. Alternatively, share with guests as an offering of hospitality, inviting them to experience peace and calm as they share the magic of the present moment with you. Double the ingredients for a larger portion size.

SERVES 1

2 slices cucumber for peace and healing

1 sprig rosemary for a clear mind

4 dashes nonalcoholic lavender bitters (such as All The Bitter) (optional) for peace and purification

1 ounce Honey Syrup (page 199 in the appendix)

½ ounce freshly squeezed lemon juice for joy and purification

2 ounces chilled Jasmine Green Tea (page 200 in the appendix) for the conscious mind

Cucumber peel and/or edible flower, for garnish

1 In your shaker, place the cucumber for rejuvenation and the rosemary for peace. Sprinkle in the relaxing bitters. As you add each ingredient, notice its calming, soothing aromatics.

2 Add the syrup to soothe. Muddle the cucumber and rosemary into the syrup.

3 Add the lemon juice to cleanse, plus the tea for the conscious mind and spirituality. Add ice and shake.

4 Tight strain into a coupe and garnish.

BEYOND THE GLASS

The Japanese tea ceremony teaches us to honor the moment, for it can never fully be recaptured. Like the jasmine flower opening with an attracting essence, the flower is a remarkable beauty but a temporary facet of nature, blossoming only for a moment in time. As you sip this drink, slow down and enjoy the moment. Observe nature, such as grass swaying in the wind. With each sip, capture another facet of this moment in time, knowing it can never fully be repeated.

AFFIRMATIONS TO SIP BY:
I am present in this moment of transition.
I trust in my inner moon and intuition to guide me.
I am exactly where I need to be and will be ready when the time is right.

MOON METAMORPHOSIS

Rest, Spiritual Insight, Transition

Tune in to your inner guidance with this dreamy, blue butterfly pea flower latte. Like a caterpillar crafting a cocoon, there are times when one must pull their energy within and transform. With its blue hue and color-changing properties, butterfly pea flower is a natural ingredient to echo the energy of such times. Associated with the planet Venus, this floral ingredient grants this recipe stunning color and supportive feminine energy and spirituality. Spices like cardamom enhance loving energies, while cinnamon, clove, and nutmeg stir spiritual insight. With subtle maple syrup as a flavorful reminder of grounded tree roots to keep you steady, and creamy coconut milk, this is a sip to nurture your spirit.

SERVES 1

1 tablespoon butterfly pea flower for transformation

⅛ teaspoon ground cardamom for loving energy

⅛ teaspoon ground clove for comfort

⅛ teaspoon ground cinnamon

⅛ teaspoon ground nutmeg

½ cup hot water

½–1 ounce maple syrup

2–3 ounces warm coconut milk

¼ teaspoon vanilla extract (optional) for peace

¼ cup additional milk, for foam top (optional)

1 Place the butterfly pea flower in a mug. Atop it, sprinkle your spices with intention—cardamom for self-love, clove for comfort, and cinnamon and nutmeg for raising spiritual vibrations.

2 Pour in the water and steep for 5 minutes, allowing it to capture the deep blue hue of the butterfly pea flower like a tea.

3 After 5 minutes, strain the tea and stir in the maple syrup (add more to taste) for grounding energy. Stir in the coconut milk and optional vanilla extract, saying whichever affirmation resonates with you.

4 If desired, top with whisked coconut milk or cream for a foam and place a dried butterfly pea flower in a crescent moon shape, a symbol of new beginnings and hope. Sip while reflecting on the following "Beyond the Glass."

BEYOND THE GLASS

During winter, all of life pulls its energy within. Trees, having let go of all their leaves in the fall, reserve their energy rather than pushing for new growth. The iris bulb awaits, slumbering beneath the snow until the right conditions to sprout forth. And while the nights might be longer, the moon's light shines brighter—a symbol of tuning in to our inner compass. How can you rest and tune within at this time, to pave the way for new growth when the time is right?

AFFIRMATIONS TO SIP BY:
I open my mind to greater wisdom.
I trust in my higher self.
Insight flows with ease.

MATCHA MOON-TINI

The Mind, Wisdom, Longevity

Open your mind with this maple matcha and cream nonalcoholic martini. With matcha for an awakening tea but grounded with soothing maple syrup, this creamy green elixir is simple to put together in just a few minutes! Fresh sage sparks the mind and spiritual wisdom, boosted by renewing mint. And coconut brings the nurturing energy of the moon. This is a great sip for something a tad more luscious but still insightful and awakening—perfect for a lunar card reading or special psychic occasion. If not using nonalcoholic amaretto, you can opt to double the recipe to your desired size.

SERVES 1

2 leaves fresh sage for wisdom

3 leaves fresh mint for the mind

½ ounce maple syrup

2 ounces Matcha (page 200 in the appendix) for harmonious, awakening energy

½ ounce coconut milk for the moon

1 ounce nonalcoholic amaretto (optional)

1 In your shaker, place the sage and mint. Drizzle the maple syrup to ground and soothe, then add the matcha for the mind as well as the nurturing coconut milk. Add nonalcoholic amaretto, if using.

2 Add ice and shake, then strain into a coupe. As you sip, say any affirmations that resonate. If desired, you can top with additional frothed cream for layered effect.

BEYOND THE GLASS

In the founding legend of tea dating from 2737 BCE,[11] mythological emperor Seng Nong fell asleep under a tree while boiling water to purify it. He had been ill and was endlessly investigating the curative properties of various plants. When he awoke, some of the tree leaves had fallen into his cup. Upon tasting it, he found the properties amazing, and thus tea was discovered—the cure he sought had been there all along. Through this legend, we can glean several lessons, but one is especially key: Sometimes the wisdom and spiritual medicine we seek are a matter of openness and receptivity, rather than forcing. In our modern day, we continuously push forward to make things fit. But by resting and resetting our minds, the right wisdom can often "drift" down from higher consciousness. As you sip this recipe, allow its mind-opening properties to reset and awaken your mind to new possibilities.

AFFIRMATIONS TO SIP BY:
Clear, compassionate thoughts fill my mind.
I invite clarity with love.
I open my mind to supportive insight from my spirit guides.

ROSE AND ROSEMARY LONDON FOG

Clarity, Psychic Abilities, Love

Clear your mind for insight and awaken your energy with this Rose and Rosemary London Fog. Black tea brings gentle energy and awakens the mind, while cream soothes and nurtures. With the additional magic of rose for love, vanilla for peace, and rosemary for clarity, this London Fog variation brings a comforting energy to uplift your spiritual senses. Subtle maple comes in at the end to lightly sweeten, adding the grounding energy of trees and the earth. This makes a perfect sip for your morning meditations, as you pull a card for the day, or when you need a nurturing sip for comfort.

SERVES 1

1 cup water

1 black tea bag (like English breakfast) for the conscious mind and energy

1 tablespoon dried food-grade rose petals for love and psychic powers

1 sprig rosemary for clarity

½ ounce maple syrup for love and longevity

⅛ teaspoon vanilla extract for peace

½ ounce half-and-half or cream of choice for nurturing and comfort

1 Set the water to boil. Meanwhile, place the tea bag and rose in a tea strainer in a mug.

2 When ready, pour the hot water over the herbs and add the rosemary for clarity (be aware that too much rosemary can cause bitterness).

3 Add the maple syrup for grounding and love and the vanilla for peace and the mind.

4 Pour in the half-and-half or cream of choice with intention, saying any affirmation that resonates.

5 Stir with the rosemary sprig for clarity, while thinking on the query at hand.

BEYOND THE GLASS

On the day of the fall equinox, all of life is held in a temporary balance. The hours of daylight are as equal as possible to the hours of night, but the balance will soon shift toward the dark. While for many the autumn equinox is a day of balance, it is also about loss and letting go—offering reflection into our spirit. As you pour the nurturing cream (bringing a balance between light and dark in the recipe), think on what you're nurturing, healing, or releasing this fall to winter season. If leaving the black tea loose leaf, you can divine insight through tasseography (page 146).

BLOOD MOON MIMOSA

Sacrifice, Psychic Abilities, the Life Cycle, Ancestors

Celebrate the mysticism of the blood moon with this pomegranate, apple, and maple mimosa that echoes its appearance and energy. With frozen pomegranate or blood orange spheres to represent the blood moon, the drink gradually turns blood red (like the moon). In fact, the meaning of the ingredients matches the occasion too—apple is a magical ingredient commonly used for the dead but also has a five-pointed star symbolic of magic when cut in half; maple sweetens this bewitching recipe, in essence a tree "blood." With anise and clove spices, it will open your mind's eye. Whether you're celebrating a total lunar eclipse turning the moon blood red or the full moon of October, it's a time of magic where the veil feels thin. This recipe will help you reflect on these themes or connect to and honor the dead while raising spiritual vibrations for spirit communication.

AFFIRMATIONS TO SIP BY:

Life and death are a cycle; all is reborn anew.

I heed wisdom and insight from the other side.

I am grateful for those who have come before me and will come after me.

recipe continued on page 142

SERVES 1

Pomegranate or blood orange juice for sacrifice

⅛ teaspoon ground clove for vibration raising

Pinch of anise seed for psychic abilities

½ ounce maple syrup

2 ounces apple juice for wisdom and magic

1 ounce freshly squeezed lemon juice

2 ounces nonalcoholic sparkling white wine

Anise star, for garnish

1 Freeze pomegranate juice into a spherical mold. If not freezing but adding it directly to the recipe, use 1 ounce per drink.

2 In your shaker, place the clove and anise seed for vibration raising and spirit communication.

3 Breathe in the essence of these mind-opening spices and add the maple syrup for tree's blood. Say any affirmations now.

4 Add the apple juice, lemon juice, and clear ice (not the pomegranate spheres) and shake.

5 Place the frozen juice sphere into a coupe. Then strain the drink into the glass.

6 Add the sparkling wine. The frozen juice should melt over time, adding a red color akin to the moon turning red.

7 Garnish with an anise star, like the star of the celestial backdrop of the moon, and sip while reflecting on what this blood moon brings you.

BEYOND THE GLASS

The namesake of this drink—the blood moon—is commonly used to refer either to the seasonal moon during October (or April in the Southern Hemisphere) or to the moon turning red during a total lunar eclipse. These seasonal monthly moons often carry names that reflect their meaning, and the blood moon is about sacrifice, ancestors, and reflection on the life and death cycle (and a perfect lunation for Samhain!). Samhain is the cross-quarter day that occurs halfway between the autumn equinox and the winter solstice. It is also the last harvest and a day to honor the dead. In combination with the blood moon, it can be about the sacrifice necessary to sustain life, or even connecting to ancestors. And in its lunar eclipse form, the blood moon is also a time of immense personal change—an opportunity for shadow work and personal alchemy.

APPLE HARVEST TEA

Gratitude, Abundance, Wisdom, Balance

Express gratitude and foster inner balance with this smoked cinnamon, maple, and oolong tea mocktail. Oolong means "black dragon," and creating this tea involves cultivation from the earth and the skill to land just the right amount of oxidation between green and black tea. It is drunk to inspire wisdom, balance, and deeper wisdom within oneself. Complemented with harvest apples—used for love magic and abundance, a perfect symbol of gratitude and the harvest season—and with smoked cinnamon for raising vibrations, this drink is perfect for intentionality, sending prayers, and celebrating abundance. Rose furthers the expression of love, and maple brings connection to trees and earth magic. Enjoy this libation in celebrating the abundance, connecting to gratitude for Mother Earth, or fostering the balance and harmony of energies within oneself for deeper wisdom.

For nonalcoholic spirit subs, I recommend Lyre's Reserve for more balanced notes or Lyre's American Malt for caramel notes instead of oolong tea.

AFFIRMATIONS TO SIP BY:

I am grateful for the earth and her abundance.

I harmonize different parts of my being into balance.

I cultivate deeper wisdom and insight.

recipe continued on page 145

SERVES 1

1 cinnamon stick
for spiritual energy

¾ ounce maple syrup
for grounding and love

6 drops rose water (optional)

½ ounce apple juice
for harvest and abundance

1½ ounces oolong tea
for inner wisdom

Large ice cube, for serving

1 ounce freshly squeezed lemon juice

1 Light the end of your cinnamon stick while thinking on your gratitude for the earth and its abundance. Then, blow out any flame and place your glass upside down over it on a fire-safe surface, such as a cutting board. The smoke should begin to fill the glass.

2 In a separate container/glass, mix the maple syrup for grounding, the rose water, if using, for love and gratitude, and the apple juice for abundance. Add the tea for inner wisdom and stir.

3 Add a big ice cube to your smoked glass, then pour in your combined ingredients. Lastly, add the lemon juice—its bright color is a stark contrast to the tea mixture, a symbol of balance between dark and light.

4 Light one end of the cinnamon stick while saying any affirmations that resonate and to send spiritual prayers. Use the unsmoked end to garnish the drink and stir while sipping in gratitude and reflection.

BEYOND THE GLASS

Midway between the summer solstice and fall equinox, Lammas (also called Lughnasadh) is also the first harvest of harvest season. It celebrates the first fruits of labor of the summer sun and signals the coming descent into fall. It is about giving gratitude to the earth for the abundance to come. Part of manifesting is also about being in tune with the flow of energy and thus the energy of the earth. Taking the time to give gratitude and connect to this energy is a form of manifestation and harmony magic for many people. While sipping, reflect on what you are grateful for and the interrelated relationship between you, sustenance, and the earth.

DIVINING with YOUR DRINK: TASSEOGRAPHY

Beyond the spiritual and ritualistic history of tea, there is another magical opportunity waiting just beneath your fingertips (or tongue) with magical mocktails: tea leaf reading. Tasseography is the art of reading tea leaves or even coffee grounds. Through interpreting the symbols the tea leaves leave behind in your glass, you can divine spiritual information. This is a great way to not just enjoy a ritualistic drink but use it to fortune-tell. That being said, this is a highly intuitive and subjective art. Relax and allow your mind to see and interpret symbols, and with practice you will develop a stronger sense for the meanings over time. Luckily, sipping tea and magical mocktails is meditative to begin with, so psychic insight may come easier!

TO PERFORM TASSEOGRAPHY:

1 Use a wide-brimmed cup, such as a traditional teacup, to get a better reading. You will also need a paper towel.

2 Decide how you want to read the leaves based on the positioning of the cup. There are many different ways to divine the tea leaves, and it is up to you which is best. This way, before you even sip, you communicate to your subconscious and guides what each area of the cup represents. While cups do exist pre-marked for this purpose, there's no need to break out the extra bucks. Here are some ways you can decipher areas of the cup:

Past, Present, Future: With the handle being held to the left, you can symbolize the bottom center of the cup as the present, what remains on the left toward the handle as the past, and what is on the right as the future.

What's Coming in and What's Leaving: Alternatively, you can read what's on the left as what's coming into your life and what's on the right as what is leaving. Or things on the lip of the cup closest to where you sip may be things that are coming your way.

Astrology: You can even match your teacup up to the twelve houses of astrology. The twelve houses represent areas of the sky that relate to various aspects of your life, such as career, romance, and so on. You can use a reference image online to guide your reading based on what falls in each area of the cup.

Or simply relax and discern whatever symbols come through, even as relative to their placement together. Some also use the plate or towel they toss the extra tea leaves onto for divination as well.

3 Then make your drink and leave the tea leaves loose. Drink each sip with an intention in mind or say it before sipping. Allow the drink to calm and open your third eye.

4 When only a small amount of tea remains, ask your query aloud and swirl the cup clockwise at least three times with the question in the front of your mind.

5 Then toss out the remaining liquid as an offering to spirit onto the paper towel. This will discard most of the tea leaves, but some should remain.

6 Unattached, examine the cup and see what you notice. Where in the cup does the sediment stay? Are some leaves farther from or closer to you? Do some clump together, and are some scattered? From this information and what you decided the various areas of the cup mean, allow a story to form. Notate and take a picture, so you can continue to reference and refine your skills over time. Since many drinks use tea, by leaving the tea loose leaf in your recipe, you can do this with many mindful sips.

AFFIRMATIONS TO SIP BY:
Like the moon, I learn to release, heal, and renew.
I allow space for forgiveness.
I release what no longer serves me and create space for healing.

LUNAR HEALING

Healing, Purification, Release

Allow the ever-changing lunar tides to cleanse and mend old wounds with this aloe, grapefruit, and rose sea salt mocktail. Through the moon's phases, she reminds us to grow, shine, release, and rest. While often the emphasis is put on manifestation and growth, they can also illuminate areas for healing. With ingredients to hydrate but also mend, this recipe is a perfect addition to lunar healing and release rituals. Sea salt helps ground, while grapefruit juice and coconut water invite lunar attunement and spiritual purification. With a spiked exterior but healing interior inside, aloe is great for both boundaries and healing. And rose honey helps soothe and bring in healing love. Altogether, this rejuvenating elixir is perfect for tuning in to the moon's ability to heal.

SERVES 1

Sea salt, for rim

Pinch of salt

½ ounce aloe gel for healing

½ ounce Rose-Honey or Honey Syrup (page 199 in the appendix) for love

1–2 ounces freshly squeezed grapefruit juice

1 ounce coconut water

1 ounce Lyre's White Cane Spirit and ½ ounce more honey syrup (optional)

1. Rim a martini glass with sea salt.
2. In your shaker, sprinkle the salt to cleanse, while saying any affirmation that resonates.
3. Then add the aloe gel for soothing wounds, followed by the syrup to bring supportive energy and self-love.
4. Add the grapefruit juice to cleanse and uplift, the coconut water for lunar purification, and the optional nonalcoholic spirit.
5. Add ice, shake, and strain into your glass.

BEYOND THE GLASS

The moon illuminates our psychic senses but also the realm of our emotions. In Western astrology, these themes are only emphasized: The moon is seen to relate to the subconscious, our sense of feeling (both intuitive and emotional), dreams, and much more. Reflecting the sun's light and changing form, illuminating the night, the moon is similarly like an internal compass, reflecting and highlighting our own subconscious wounds. These feelings have wisdom: it's not just an emotional high but can reveal more if we listen. Tune in to what is revealed to you during the full moon—what is the moon illuminating to heal and release? What is it time to let go of?

MOON GODDESS COLADA

Intuition, Spiritual Purification, Hope

Just like the moon changes shape—waxing, waning, and vanishing only to reappear anew—nurturing the spirit can revive one's inner light in the darkest of times. This Moon Goddess Colada evokes the healing, rejuvenating powers of the moon using cucumbers and coconut milk, instead of the more common, but processed, store-bought cream of coconut. The cucumber evokes the moon's calming and rejuvenating energy, while the coconut milk taps into the moon's powers of intuition and spirituality. Combined with jovial pineapple, refreshing mint to clear the mind, and the reawakening properties of yuzu, this creamy, addictive, and hydrating cucumber mint colada renews hope and uplifts your spirit. You'll receive the immune-boosting and digestive health benefits of the coconut, pineapple, and yuzu too! A perfect example of how catering to our spirit can transmute our heart, mind, and body.

AFFIRMATIONS TO SIP BY:

Like the moon waxes from dark to light, the hope within me grows bright.

I embody physical and spiritual renewal.

I am attuned to the spiritual, intuitive wisdom of my inner moon.

recipe continued on page 152

SERVES 1

3 mint leaves for refreshing the senses

2 slices cucumber for the moon, peace, and rejuvenation

⅓ ounce agave

1 ounce coconut milk for the moon, intuition, and spiritual purification

¼ ounce grapefruit juice for positivity

1 ounce pineapple juice

¼ ounce freshly squeezed lime juice for cleansing **or yuzu juice** for renewal

1 ounce nonalcoholic tequila or coconut rum (optional)

Edible flower or pineapple wedge and pineapple leaf, for garnish

1 In your shaker, place the mint, cucumber, and agave. Thinking on what weighs you down and releasing that, muddle the mint and cucumber into the sweetening, soothing agave.

2 Add the coconut milk, grapefruit, pineapple, and lime juices, and the nonalcoholic replacement, if using.

3 Add ice and shake, thinking on what you are transforming. Strain and pour over ice into your desired glass, like refilling your own spiritual cup.

4 Garnish and enjoy, as you refresh your hope, mind, and spirit with each sip!

* *For added magic, you can create beautiful blue ice cubes (as pictured) that will transition to purple upon contact with citrus, using butterfly pea flower. To do so, steep 1 tablespoon dried butterfly pea flower in 1 cup hot water for up to 10 minutes (for a rich deep blue color). Freeze into ice cubes, then blend into crushed ice to strain the drink into at the end. You can leave the lime or yuzu for very last, for a color-change transition.*

BEYOND THE GLASS

The ancient Aztecs believed that the maguey (or agave) plant was reborn from the body of the goddess Mayahuel following a tale of love, passion, and death. A fertility goddess with nurturing qualities, her story of rebirth in plant form shows how we can be born anew. As you sip this nurturing drink, think of the magic of agave reigniting your own inner passion.

ROSE of REMEMBRANCE

Memories, Love, Wisdom, Healing

Connect with fond memories, remember loved ones, and heal the past with this rose, anise, and pomegranate mocktail for remembrance. Our stories and journeys, regardless of whether they were happy, often influence who we are. While we rise above them, these memories carry wisdom and insight. When healed, we can manifest a better future and expand our perspective. Empowered with ingredients for remembrance, healing, and ancestry, this is a drink to remind us of our stories and roots—and perhaps even connect with those who have passed on. Rose tea brings love and spiritual elevation, while pomegranate and apple connect to healing and the dead. As the sweetener, maple syrup brings loving energy and longevity but also a reminder of tree roots, our own heritage, and family trees that ground our experiences. Anise comes in lightly, bringing an herbal balance, purifying energy, and inviting communication with spirits. This is a great sip for remembering loved ones, helping heal the inner child, and transforming memories into wisdom. You can also add the pomegranate juice last for a layered effect.

AFFIRMATIONS to SIP BY:

I honor the insight of my ancestors.

I am grateful for the wisdom of my experiences.

I heal and create space for new memories.

recipe continued on page 155

SERVES 1

1 slice fresh apple for love, healing, and magic

⅓ ounce maple syrup for love and longevity

1 sprig rosemary, plus an extra, for garnish for remembrance

⅛ teaspoon ground anise for spirit communication

½ ounce pomegranate juice for death

½ ounce freshly squeezed lemon juice

1½ ounces Rose Tea (page 200 in the appendix) for love, psychic powers, and healing

1 In your shaker place the apple, a nurturing ingredient, reminiscent of trees. Add the maple syrup for the grounding energy of ancestors, a sprig of rosemary, and sprinkle the anise for spirit communication and psychic insight.

2 Muddle these together, thinking of your own life's journey. Say any affirmations that speak to you.

3 Add the pomegranate juice for Persephone's descent into the underworld, the lemon juice for cleansing, and the tea for healing. Add ice and shake.

4 Strain into a coupe. Light the tip of the second rosemary sprig for remembrance and garnish.

BEYOND THE GLASS

Persephone was a young Greek goddess associated with spring and the daughter of harvest and fertility goddess Demeter. She was stolen away to the underworld by Hades, and while there she ate pomegranate seeds. Because of this, when Zeus settled the matter, it was decided that Persephone would remain Queen of the Underworld half the year but spend the other half with her mother aboveground. This gave way to the seasons—six months of the year the earth would be fertile and the other six desolate as Demeter mourned her daughter. Because of this myth, many like to use pomegranate to connect to the dead. But it is also a fruit of fertility, wealth, wishes, and creativity. It is a symbol of where there is death or stolen innocence, there is also rejuvenation. It showcases how, going through our shadow side, we can reclaim our power from the past.

CHALICES AND the TAROT

What mystical imagery is complete without a crystal ball or card deck? From pulling a daily "card" to doing a new- or full-moon reading, the tarot plays a key role in modern mysticism. It is a way to connect to the divine for advice or use the power of symbolism to communicate with the subconscious or spirit guides for insight. The tarot specifically is a divination method using seventy-eight cards with various signs and symbols depicting core archetypes and elements of the universal human experience. They are broken down into twenty-two major arcana cards that express major life events and fifty-six minor arcana broken into four suites of the classical elements.

The tarot can be a powerful way to communicate with your subconscious for insight or to get advice from your spirit guides. And just like we talked about the powerful symbol of the vessel, the glass or chalices play an important role in the symbolism of the tarot. Through both the major arcana and the cups suite, we can glean a deeper meaning of the power and potential of what you put in your glass. Here are some core chalice-themed cards you will find in the tarot deck, to help you attune to the symbolic, spiritual power of what you drink.

- The **STAR** card depicts a naked woman kneeling, with one foot on land and one in water. Above her bowed head shine one large and seven small stars. She holds in each hand a vessel held out to either side, from which she pours liquid onto both the pond and the land. Behind her, a lush scene grows. Generally, the Star card symbolizes hope, faith, purpose, renewal, and spirituality. But through pouring nurturing, life-giving liquid on both water (the classic element that symbolizes emotion and intuition) and earth (the physical), new life grows. It is symbolic of when divinely aligned and true to our spirit, whatever we pour our energy into and nurture from a place of authenticity can grow and thrive.
- In the **TEMPERANCE** card, an angel stands at the edge of a body of water (again, one foot on land, one on water). Behind them on one side is a mountain and the sun, tall grass with flowers on the other. In their hands, they pour liquid from one cup to another. The card symbolizes balance, moderation, patience, and purpose.

The flowing of water from one cup to another showcases alchemy and the balancing flow between two cups.

- CUPS SUITE—The entire cups suite of the tarot relates to the element of water and is seen to represent themes along the lines of emotion, the heart, intuition, and love. Here are some specific cards:
- ACE OF CUPS—An outstretched hand with a chalice resting upon it overflows with water that falls to a still ocean-like landscape scattered with water lilies or lotus flowers. The card is an indicator of new beginnings and potential in the realm of emotion and feeling, whether it be love or spirituality. A dove dives toward the cup. It is symbolic of potential, new beginnings, and divine blessings flowing in to nourish emotion and spirit.
- TWO OF CUPS—A couple face each other, each with a chalice outstretched as though to share each other's drinks. This card symbolizes the sharing of nurturing energy or emotional connection with another. Alternatively, it can relate to something (rather than someone) that feeds your spirit and emotions as equally as you give to it. It is symbolic of emotional connection, equal give and take, or attraction, unity, reciprocity, and authenticity within relationships.
- THREE OF CUPS—Three women move in a tight-knit circle, their arms reaching up to clink glasses in the air. This card is symbolic of celebration and teamwork—an alignment of forces or collaboration that brings success, joy, and fulfillment.
- FOUR OF CUPS—A man sits beneath a tree on a green landscape. Before him are four cups: three resting on the lush earth, one held up to him in offering by an ethereal hand. The man's arms are crossed, his head bent down in thought. The card depicts a possible sense of dissatisfaction, that what has been offered or is available is not what the person wants. It could be about missing or denying opportunities or, conversely, reevaluating and contemplation.
- QUEEN OF CUPS—A woman is seated on a throne at the edge of a body of water. With both arms, she stretches a fancy chalice out toward the water, her eyes closed and head bowed in focus. The card is symbolic of receptivity, empathy, and intuition—a sense of connecting to something greater for spiritual wisdom.

Those are just a few cards of the Cups suite. Through these cards, we can glean the symbolism contained within the chalice: the potential to not just celebrate but also share, exchange, and nurture the body, emotions, and intuition.

AFFIRMATIONS TO SIP BY:

The sun will rise again.

I persist, persevere, and evolve.

I embrace inspiration and wisdom in every challenge.

DESERT BLOSSOM

Perseverance, Beauty, Wisdom, Healing

Sip in the wisdom of the desert with this smoky dragon fruit, orange, and agave mocktail. Despite the hot and dry landscape, life finds a way to survive in the heat—cacti reserve their water and bear fruit in the spring; agave perseveres and blooms after decades; desert sage, a plant symbolic of wisdom, purification, and longevity, thrives. Inspired by the lessons of the desert, this drink utilizes pink dragon fruit, sage, aloe, and agave for a mystical mixture of healing, wisdom, and perseverance. Layered with orange on top and a light pink dragon fruit base for the inspiring desert sunsets, you'll find the wisdom and strength needed within.

SERVES 1

Smoky salt, for rim for grounding

3 slices dragon fruit, divided

3 sage leaves for longevity and wisdom

1–2 drops liquid smoke (optional)

½ ounce agave for rebirth

¼ ounce aloe gel for healing

1 ounce freshly squeezed lime juice

1 ounce nonalcoholic tequila replacement (optional)

1 ounce soda water

2 ounces freshly squeezed orange juice for inspiration

Sage sprig, for garnish

1. Prepare the rim of your glass with salt, a symbol of grounding and protection.
2. In your shaker, place two of the slices of dragon fruit and the sage for cleansing. Drop in the liquid smoke for a smoky essence, then the agave for the flower's nectar, and muddle. Be sure to firmly muddle the dragon fruit skin to get the pink color.
3. Add the aloe for healing and the lime juice to cleanse, then add any nonalcoholic spirits, if using, and ice. Shake, using the movement to shake off any woes or worries.
4. Strain over ice into the glass, add the soda water (if using), and top with the orange juice for a layered effect.
5. Garnish with the remaining dragon fruit slice and sage sprig. While sipping, savor the sunset and say any affirmations that speak to you.

BEYOND THE GLASS

The desert is a harsh landscape filled with beauty and inspiration. Spiked cacti produce pink prickly pear and a home for desert birds. Monsoon season brings lightning storms and turns a rare rain into dangerous flash floods—but leaves the land replenished. Unique life and beauty thrive in these environments. While you may be going through a tough time, these serve as a reminder that it is possible to persevere and that an even rarer beauty can flourish.

AFFIRMATIONS TO SIP BY:

Like the full moon aglow in the dark of night, I open to intuitive insight.

I heed the wisdom of my inner compass and find deeper healing.

I'm receptive to the infinite spiritual wisdom of the universe.

SELENE'S SEER SOUR

Intuition, Spirituality, Purification

Lift your spirits and tune in to the moon's wisdom with this butterfly pea flower, lavender, and grapefruit tea mocktail. The moon is often a source of psychic inspiration—radiating in the dark of night and illuminating our emotions. It brings things to the surface and is a powerful time for healing and intuition. Inspired by the mystical magic of this time, this floral tea recipe will uplift your energy but also invite introspection. For lunar energy, you can add ½ ounce coconut water.

SERVES 1

3 ounces hot water

½ tablespoon butterfly pea flower for transformation and spirituality

1 teaspoon dried rose petals for psychic powers and divination

½ ounce Lavender-Agave Syrup (page 199 in the appendix) for psychic abilities

1½ ounces fresh grapefruit juice for purification

Sprig of lavender or rosemary, for garnish

1. Set the hot water to boil.
2. In a mug, place the butterfly pea flower for spirituality and color-changing magic. Add the rose petals and pour in the hot water, a metaphor for filling your cup. Let steep for 5–10 minutes, chill, and add to a shaker.
3. Pour in the syrup, add ice, shake, and strain into a coupe or martini glass.
4. Say any affirmations that resonate and pour in the grapefruit juice to uplift your spirit, noticing the color change—a visual shift in energy.
5. Garnish, lightly burning the tip of a sprig of lavender or rosemary for clearing smoke to help provide psychic vision.

BEYOND THE GLASS

Butterfly pea flower changes color upon contact with acid. With the added citrus, this drink changes the color from blue to purple-pink. Use the opportunity of the visual color change to help bring transformation or insight in your own light. As you add the grapefruit, think on what your question or query is and allow the color change to symbolize your third eye opening to wisdom, using the smoke garnish to discern shapes and symbols.

WARMING WHITE WINE

Spiritual Connection, Love, Psychic Powers

In our spiritual journey, we often seek comfort through our connection to spirit, to guide the way for healing. Inspired by that very intention, this nonalcoholic white mulled wine uses allspice, cardamom, anise, and soothing maple to connect to the wisdom and healing power of spirit. Through dealcoholized or alcohol-removed white wine, the spiritual symbolism of grapes is accented by healing apple for magic, wisdom, and gratitude for Earth's gift. Optional orange slices can be added for luck and to inspire joy. A sprinkle of allspice invites healing energy, and cardamom and rose are used for love and psychic power. Star-shaped star anise serves as a reminder for connection to spirit while infusing clarifying properties. Altogether, this spiritually spiced, warming wine will nurture your spirit as much as it does the stomach. You can also chill the infusion afterward to serve sangria-style.

AFFIRMATIONS TO SIP BY:

My connection to spirit brings me comfort, guidance, and warmth.

I am grateful for the abundant wisdom of the universe that guides me.

I connect to the nurturing, loving energy of my spirit guides.

recipe continued on page 164

SERVES 5 OR 6

1 bottle nonalcoholic white wine (such as sauvignon blanc)

6 horizontally cut slices apple for love and wisdom

1 teaspoon ground allspice for healing

½ teaspoon ground cardamom for love

1 tablespoon dried rose petals for love and healing

4 slices orange (optional) for inspiration

6 tablespoons maple syrup for love and grounding

4 anise stars, plus 1 additional for each mug, for garnish for purification and spirit

1 In a pot over medium heat, place the alcohol-removed wine. Add the apples—sliced to reveal their star-shaped center—a reminder of the loving, healing energy of spirit.

2 Sprinkle in the allspice for healing, the cardamom for comfort, and the rose petals for love and psychic healing.

3 Add the orange slices, if using, for a general sense of uplifting. Then stir in the maple syrup for the grounding, loving energy of earth. Add the star anise for spirit connection, a guiding star (alongside the apple) of spirit to lead the way. Stir the mixture, saying any affirmations that resonate.

4 Bring to a boil, then reduce to low heat and simmer for 10–15 minutes, stirring occasionally and enjoying the uplifting psychic aroma that the mixture brings to the air.

5 Remove from the heat and pour the drink into warm tempered mugs, adding a star anise per glass as a reminder of spiritual guidance.

BEYOND THE GLASS

Much of our mysticism is derived from the stars and our place within the universe. The constellations tell stories that help us find meaning, myth, and magic as we navigate life. Likewise, the North Star (Polaris) shines brightly from the Ursa Minor constellation or the Little Dipper. Finding Polaris, oriented close to our North Pole, in the sky helps navigate in the dark of the night, while the other constellations are constantly rotating. Similarly, having your own North Star can help you find your way in murky moments. While sipping this drink, reflect on what your North Star is: What keeps you centered and connected? What gives you purpose or something to keep moving toward? Use the star anise as a symbol for that. That way, regardless of astrological weather or what is happening in your life, you have your spiritual center to guide you. Once finished drinking, dry the star anise from your glass and place it under your pillow to give guidance in dreams at night. Alternatively, keep it on your person when in need of that guidance or reminder.

CHAPTER 9

MANIFESTATION

Potions for Prosperity, Success, and Mindset

What if instead of an ordinary mocktail, you had one that matched what you're working on in life right now, such as a drink for positivity or confidence? Potions don't have to be a thing of myth. What you drink your body breaks down and uses as fuel. When you sip in nutrient-rich mocktails but also use herbology and the folkloric, energetic principles to inform the ingredients, you can craft recipes that bring your body and energy into alignment with your goals.

Through the recipes in this section, you can come into energetic resonance with your desires and manifest with ease. Pave the pathway to success with drinks using ingredients associated with wealth, achievement, luck, or blessings. Open the road and brainstorm with the meditative Road-Opening Orange Toddy. Share blessings with friends with the Blessing Mimosa Bombs, followed by a bay leaf wishing spell—perfect for good luck in the New Year or a magical Sunday brunch. And because part of manifestation is also about mindset and overcoming hurdles, you will also uncover recipes and rituals for determination and motivation, like the Positivity Potion to boost your mood and bring optimism or the Blackberry Black Tea Beverage for focus and wisdom. To take your manifestation skills to the next level, you will also learn how to attract your desires with sweetening spells that correspond to your potions or heighten energy for spiritual success with spices. Making the recipes in this section can help release mental and energetic blockages along the pathway to success and help shift you toward achieving your goals.

AFFIRMATIONS TO SIP BY:

My mind and motivation are clear.

I am ready to take action toward my goals.

I am capable of achieving my dreams.

EMPOWERING EARL MULE

Action, Power, Victory

Inspire action and conquer your goals with the support of this motivating thyme and cinnamon black tea mule. With the fortifying bite of ginger beer to energize and empower, and blessings of bay leaf for victory, thyme for courage, and cranberry for action, nothing can stand in your way. This spicy, herbal nonalcoholic Moscow mule will have you buzzing with motivation and strength to take steps toward your goals. Enjoy while making an action plan or alongside confidence spells to boost belief in your dreams.

SERVES 1

1 fresh bay leaf, plus additional, for garnish for strength and success

2 sprigs thyme for courage

½ ounce agave

⅛ teaspoon ground cinnamon for success and fast luck

1 ounce freshly squeezed lime juice

4 dashes nonalcoholic orange bitters (such as All The Bitter) (optional)

1 ounce Earl grey or black tea for energy and vitality

2 ounces ginger beer for success and power

½ ounce cranberry juice for action and goals

1 ounce nonalcoholic whiskey replacement, such as Lyre's Traditional Reserve (optional)

Cinnamon stick, for garnish

1. Hold the bay leaf while thinking on your intention. Say any affirmations that appeal to you now. If desired, you can lightly burn the bay leaf for wishes—since it is fresh, it won't burn all the way through, but it can add a smoky flavor to this drink by doing so. Drop into glass or mug.
2. Add the thyme and agave to your cup and sprinkle in the cinnamon while thinking on your intention. Muddle these ingredients together.
3. Add the lime juice to remove blockages and the bitters, if using, to help open the road and for luck.
4. Add the tea for energy and the successful themes of bergamot, then add ice and the ginger beer. Add the cranberry juice, for action and goals, and optional nonalcoholic spirits.
5. Garnish with the cinnamon stick (or bay leaves, for victory), to stir with intention.

BEYOND THE GLASS

This mocktail is designed to help you make steps toward your goals. Likewise, the stone carnelian can help you act. Since ancient times, this vibrant orange-red crystal was thought to infuse courage in the wearer. By holding the stone while you sip and envisioning your goals (you can even keep it in a bag with dried thyme and cinnamon sticks) and keeping it on your person, you can help inspire motivation and action toward your aims.

AFFIRMATIONS TO SIP BY:

Positive energy radiates from every cell in my body.

With each sip, I soak in sunlight.

My inner joy and inspiration shine as vibrantly as the sun.

POSITIVITY POTION

Positivity, Happiness, Peace, Inspiration

Sip in some liquid sunlight with this cardamom and chamomile elixir. With ingredients to inspire joy, calm, and a positive outlook, this Positivity Potion is just the drink to uplift your spirit or share a smile with a friend. Lavender and chamomile inspire peace and calm, allowing you to relax. A pinch of ground cardamom invokes loving, warm energy to soothe your spirit. Lemon, orange, and ginger uplift and energize. With ingredients associated with peace and positivity, this potion is sure to put a smile on your face.

SERVES 1

2 slices fresh ginger

1 ounce Honey Syrup (page 199 in the appendix) for happiness

⅛ teaspoon ground cardamom for love

4 drops nonalcoholic lavender bitters (such as All The Bitter) for peace

2 ounces Chamomile Tea (page 199 in the appendix) for calm

1 ounce freshly squeezed lemon juice for friendship and happiness

1 ounce freshly squeezed orange juice for joy

1 ounce Lyre's White Cane Spirit (optional)

Chamomile flower or orange peel, for garnish

1 In your glass, place the ginger and syrup. Muddle the ginger to express its powerful, energizing bite for success.

2 Sprinkle the cardamom, for mood-boosting and bringing loving energy.

3 Add the bitters and pour in the tea for peace and relaxation. Add the lemon juice, orange juice, optional nonalcoholic spirit, and ice, and garnish.

BEYOND THE GLASS

The summer solstice marks the beginning of summer and the longest day of the year. While the hours in the day remain the same throughout the year, those that belong to the day and those that belong to the night vary. The solstice has the most hours of daylight that there will be in a year. And the months that follow are filled with abundance and harvest. With the increase in sunlight, there's naturally more vitamin D in our systems—we can get more done, feel more joyful, or connect with friends. Summer is a reminder of finding our inner light, sense of positivity, and joy. Regardless of whether you are celebrating summer or just reflecting on summer energy to inspire your inner light, contemplate: What are the things that bring you happiness or contentment? What ignites your inner light or warms your spirit, just like the sun? How can you fill your metaphorical cup with more joy?

AFFIRMATIONS TO SIP BY:
Abundance flows in my finances, friendships, and life.
I manifest money with ease.
I am grateful for the abundance and blessings coming my way.

ABUNDANT BLACKBERRY MONEY MOCKTAIL

Money, Abundance, Love

Sip in money magic with this blackberry, basil, and chamomile elixir. An unexpected pairing with chamomile, this juicy and tantalizing recipe will energize your money magic abilities and is easily addictive. Blackberry enlivens, a symbol of abundance. Chamomile is often used in money magic, but it also brings solar energy and peace—helping to remove any anxieties that may be blocking your success with finances. Basil brings mental clarity, abundance, and love, while cinnamon blesses for fast luck in manifestation. With summer-fall flavors celebrating the abundance of the harvest season, this is a drink filled with money, happiness, love, and hard work—a perfect accompaniment for harvest celebration, rituals, or money magic.

SERVES 1

3 blackberries for luck and money

3 basil leaves

⅛ teaspoon ground cinnamon for success and fast luck

1 ounce maple syrup for money

4 ounces Chamomile Tea (page 199 in the appendix) for money

1 ounce freshly squeezed lime juice

1 ounce nonalcoholic gin replacement, such as Lyre's London Dry (optional)

Extra-large basil leaf, blackberries, and cinnamon stick, for garnish

1 In the bottom of your cup, place the blackberries, a ripe symbol of the summer's abundance, luscious like your pockets are about to be!

2 Add the green basil, like the green of your incoming money. Sprinkle the cinnamon for fast luck. Pour in the maple syrup for abundance of trees and longevity in money. Muddle while saying any affirmation that appeals to you.

3 Add the tea and lime juice to cleanse. Pour in optional nonalcoholic spirit and stir clockwise while thinking on what you're manifesting as you mix. Then add ice and garnish.

BEYOND THE GLASS

A cinnamon stick not only is a perfect wand with which to stir and garnish your drink but also can be burned as a light incense. To further the manifestive power of this potion, use the cinnamon stick as a light incense by burning the edge that sticks out of the drink. Blow out the flame while thinking of your intention and visualize the smoke that results drawing your intention toward you.

COFFEE, CLOVE, AND CINNAMON NO-TINI

Creativity, Energy, Luck, Riches

Espresso martinis are a favorite for many and for good reason. They channel the love of coffee into a decadent, elevated sip. With spiced and savory additions, this nonalcoholic coffee martini makes for a magical mocktail to inspire the mind. In addition to the traditional coffee, clove, nutmeg, and cinnamon help to raise energetic vibrations. An optional (but recommended) addition of fig preserves entices both mind and tongue, and invites prosperity. This elegant concoction will have you feeling inspired, luscious, and energized. Your creativity is sure to be stimulated as well as your ability to draw in your desires.

If you don't have an espresso machine, you can craft a close replacement by brewing 4 tablespoons ground espresso beans in ½ cup hot water in a French press. Use consistent pressure when pressing down.

AFFIRMATIONS TO SIP BY:

My mind is inspired, enticed, and energized.

I attract ideas and luck with ease.

My creativity cultivates abundance.

recipe continued on page 174

SERVES 1

Bar spoon of fig preserves (optional) for prosperity and energy

¼–½ ounce maple syrup for money

Generous pinch of ground cloves for money/riches

Generous pinch of ground nutmeg for luck and money

Generous pinch of ground cinnamon for manifestation, fast luck, and success

2 ounces espresso for energy and illuminating the mind

4 dashes nonalcoholic walnut bitters (optional) for wishes and mental powers

2 ounces nonalcoholic coffee liqueur replacement

Anise star and 3 coffee beans, for garnish

1 In your shaker, place the preserves for abundance, and the maple syrup to sweeten your desires.

2 Sprinkle in each spice, as though raining down riches. As you do, say any affirmation that appeals to you.

3 Add the espresso, bitters, if using, and nonalcoholic replacement. Add ice and shake, energizing these manifestive ingredients inside your tin. Shake extra hard to get a nice foam.

4 Double strain into a coupe and garnish.

BEYOND THE GLASS

While you can divine coffee grounds in the same way you can read tea leaves (see chapter 8), you can also divine using coffee beans. Called favomancy, this involves throwing beans and interpreting divine information by the pattern in which they fall. This usually involves a divination board or cloth to aid the process. However, you can also divine by using the three beans from your garnish. When done sipping, confirm any ideas gleaned by taking the beans into your hands. Think on your question and toss them down. Based on how many beans land with the cleaved side up or down, you can divine a yes or no answer. Alternatively, you can toss them onto a board or cloth with symbols to get more nuanced information.

PUMPKIN MOON MOCKTAIL

Nurturing Abundance, Success, Manifestation

Come autumn, few flavors are as iconic as pumpkin spice and coffee. At the same time, espresso martinis are also a famous, elegant drink. Why not combine them into a decadent drink? Nurture abundance and your energy to pursue it with this Pumpkin Moon Mocktail. Pumpkin and coconut are both associated with the moon and healing, inviting nourishing energy, while the popular pumpkin spices (that also happen to be great for manifestation in magic) and coffee energize. This is a great choice for when you want a bit of energy and motivation to assist your manifestation but are also in need of some support. Sip as a creamy, energizing treat while working or as part of a manifestation spell or lunar abundance ritual.

You can often find canned pumpkin in the baking aisle of your local grocery store. If using nonalcoholic spirits, you can order them online.

AFFIRMATIONS TO SIP BY:

The limitless energy of the universe nourishes my motivation.

The moon nurtures abundance in my life.

With each sip, I am filled with supportive energy to help me pursue my dreams.

recipe continued on page 177

SERVES 1

2 tablespoons canned pure pumpkin for abundance, goddess worship, and money

⅛ teaspoon ground cinnamon for success and power

⅛ teaspoon ground nutmeg for luck and money

⅛ teaspoon ground allspice for courage and luck

¾–1 ounce maple syrup for longevity and money

3 ounces coffee for conscious mind and physical energy

1½ ounces nonalcoholic coffee spirit

1½ ounces coconut milk or almond milk for spirituality and nurturing

Whipped coconut or heavy whipping cream, for garnish

Cinnamon stick, for garnish

1 In your shaker, place the pumpkin for abundance. Sprinkle in the spices for manifestation and success. Add the maple syrup to allure your desires to you and then the coffee for energy. Add nonalcoholic coffee spirit and milk.

2 Add ice and shake while thinking on your intention. Say any affirmations that speak to you now, while all the ingredients are alchemically mixing.

3 Pour into a glass, top with cream, and garnish.

BEYOND THE GLASS

The end of summer through the first half of fall brings harvest season. At this time, full moons play an important role—they shine well into the night, bringing much-needed light to allow harvesting late. More importantly, these moons are associated with herbs—the full moon brings the land into abundance. We often celebrate manifestation or allow the moon to reflect what we need to release. Through nurturing our intentions through the lunar cycle, we can bring things to abundance. What attributes would you like to nurture and grow within yourself or your life?

AFFIRMATIONS TO SIP BY:

Sugar and spice, with each sip I entice.

Money, luck, and love flow effortlessly my way.

I am worthy of my desires.

SUGAR AND SPICE

Attraction, Money, Love, Luck

Attraction isn't just about love and romance—it's about alluring desires of all kinds, whether abundance, blessings, or winning favors. This small, sweet and spiced potion with apricot, maple, and rose is designed to help you attract what you desire. Apricot entices, helping you to gain favor. Allspice adds a seductive warming element to the recipe while inviting luck and money. Maple subtly sweetens love and abundance your way, and a hint of orange encourages blessings and inspiration. Whether serving for love and romance or drawing in some financial luck, this attractive apricot drink is just the mocktail to help you gain favor. Serve to guests at a business event, at a heart-to-heart with an in-law, or with a manifestation spell and envision your desires coming right to you. You can also add 1 ounce nonalcoholic amaretto for a sweet treat.

SERVES 1

Spoon of apricot preserves for love, attraction, and gaining favor

Pinch of allspice for money and luck

¼–½ ounce maple syrup for love and money

4 drops rose water for alluring love

½ ounce freshly squeezed orange juice for blessings

1 ounce freshly squeezed lemon juice

½ ounce cream, such as coconut milk or half and half

Spritz of rose water

Cherries, for garnish

1 In your shaker, place the apricot, thinking on Venus/Aphrodite and her ability to attract favor with her charm.

2 Sprinkle the allspice for money and luck and sweeten with the maple syrup to ground the energy and attract abundance your way.

3 Add the rose water for the attracting essence of rose, the orange juice to uplift, the lemon juice for cleansing and joy, and the cream to soothe and nurture.

4 Add ice, shake, and strain into a Nick and Nora glass. Spritz the top with rose water to allure your desires while saying any affirmation that appeals to you and garnish.

BEYOND THE GLASS

Aphrodite, the Greek goddess of love, was known for her beauty and ability to entice. These themes are echoed through the planet Venus in astrology. However, it is important to note that Venus's domain is about not just love but the ability to attract with charm. This recipe is filled with ingredients to allure desires of all kinds. How can you allure your desires to you? What's part of your unique charm?

AFFIRMATIONS TO SIP BY:

Wherever I trek, the path is clear.

All roads and possibilities open before me.

What is aligned and in my best interest comes my way.

ROAD-OPENING ORANGE TODDY

Road Opening, Wishes, Vibration Raising

Open the road to success with this bay leaf and orange not toddy. A ritual and potion in one, you will cleanse the way forward with a cloved lemon wheel, then make a wish with a bay leaf. With empowering spices to raise your vibration and orange for luck, you will transmute blockages and bring in blessings. This spiced, warming beverage is perfect to enjoy an intentional cup while reflecting on your goals, discerning what route you want to take in life, or envisioning the possibilities of the future. Instead of whole cloves, you can also sprinkle in ⅛ teaspoon ground clove.

SERVES 1

7 ounces hot water

2 slices lemon for cleansing and positivity

14 cloves for raising vibrations

2 dried bay leaves for wishes

1 tablespoon honey or ¾ ounce maple syrup

¼ teaspoon ground cinnamon for manifestation

1 ounce freshly squeezed orange juice for blessings

1 Set the hot water to boil. Meanwhile, take the lemons and slowly insert the cloves through them. As you do so, think about what your goals are and envision the road opening to you.

2 Hold the bay leaves and see your goal come to fruition. Place them in the bottom of a mug and add the cloved lemons on top of them.

3 Pour in the honey to sweeten the way and then sprinkle the cinnamon to quicken and elevate the energy.

4 Pour in the hot water and let steep for 5–7 minutes. Then add the orange juice to help it cool as well as bless it with luck and success.

BEYOND THE GLASS

When you're done with your toddy, you might notice some leftover spices, herbs, and citrus in the bottom of your cup. Don't let those go to waste! They can be added to a simmer pot to bring the brightening, blessing energy of your intentions to your whole home. A simmer pot is when you simmer water with fragrant herbs, fruits, and spices to aromatize the home. As the water evaporates, the essence will fill the air. To do so, pour two cups of water (or moon water) into a pot and hover your hands above. Think on your intention, praying over the water. Then bring it to boil and add the leftover spices and any others you would like (perhaps other spices that have been dried, left from other drinks). Once boiling, reduce to a simmer and envision the aroma blessing your home.

SYRUPS, SUGAR JARS, AND SWEETENING SPELLS

Much in the same way that it adds an alluring quality by sweetening our drinks, sugar is also used for attraction magic. A honey jar might be used to win over a boss or an in-law or a sugar bowl to attract clients and tips. This creates the perfect opportunity to boost your manifestation skills: You can relate the sweetener and herbs you are using in your mocktail to a sweetening spell, whether attracting good luck or love. These spells employ the use of writing your intention down as a positive affirmation that reinforces your desires—and luckily, there are LOTS of those in this book! You can use the affirmation you chose for your drink in a corresponding sweetening spell. That's an even more magical way to layer, prolong, and emphasize the energy of a potion. Here are three sweetening spells you can match with the recipes in this book.

SUGAR JAR

A sugar jar is a spell in which sugar, herbs, and any other related ingredients are encapsulated in a jar for the purpose of attracting or "sweetening" a desire—whether it be a relationship, an intention, or general positive energy to a situation. It acts to "sweeten" energy much in the same way sugar does naturally. Candles are then regularly burned atop to keep the energy going. It can be a perfect spell coinciding with using simple syrup in your mocktail.

To create a sugar jar, write your intention (or chosen drink affirmation) on a piece of paper. Fill the jar halfway with sugar. For an added boost, you can add herbs aligned to your intention or match what was used in the mystical mocktail.

Fold your note with your affirmation toward you, then add it to the jar. Fill the rest of the jar with sugar and close the lid. Energetically charge the jar by burning a candle atop it, then continue to "feed" or maintain the spell by doing so once a week. Many choose Friday for its association with Venus.

HONEY JAR

A honey jar works much in the same way as a sugar jar, except (just like the viscosity of honey makes it move slower) it takes a bit longer to work. However, it gradually builds up energy and can be powerful and long lasting.

To make a honey jar, fill a jar halfway with honey. Sprinkle in any related herbs. For instance, in this book we use a honey syrup infused with rose petals. To create resonance between the energy of the spell and your potion, you can add rose petals to the jar. On a piece of paper, write the affirmation or the name of the person you want to sweeten up to you. Add it to the honey jar, along with the herbs, and fill the jar the rest of the way with honey. Close the jar and burn a candle atop it once a week, such as on a Friday.

SUGAR BOWL

A sugar bowl is an alternative form of a sweetening spell. It follows the same principles, except that it is created in a bowl and thus has a more open nature that allows you to use it like an altar to which you add items over time.

To create a sugar bowl, think on your intention and choose an affirmation from the potion recipe that speaks to you. Write it down and reflect on what ingredients match your intention, whether it's selecting ingredients similar to your drink or using the reference in the back and what you have on hand.

Place your paper on the bottom of the bowl and pour in sugar. Mix the sugar with any spices that appeal to you and add any dried flowers or crystals you desire. You can nestle them atop the bowl, mix them into it, or a bit of both. You can even sprinkle spices in symbols that speak to you for added magic.

When you have an appearance that you like, hover your hand above and envision your intention. Say your affirmation aloud and enjoy your corresponding mocktail. Continuously feed the bowl once a week by adding something to "spruce" it up, like an additional coin or dollar bill if the bowl is for money, for example.

AFFIRMATIONS TO SIP BY:
The sun invigorates my spirit.
I am energized, inspired, and motivated.
My mind is clear for decision-making, and nothing stands in my way.

ORANGE SOLAR ENERGY® ELIXIR

Energy, Hex-Breaking, Strength, Victory

Embolden your energy with the power of Mars, the sun, and the element of fire with this solar spiced elixir. With orange to excite your energy like a morning cup of OJ, ginger for vitality, turmeric, and cayenne, this elixir is sure to invigorate your senses for power and vivacity. These ingredients are also attuned to purification, helping dispel blockages to your flow of energy, such as the basil garnish, which inspires mental clarity for proper decision-making. This is an inspiring sip, a celebration of the zest of life to awaken and brighten your energy.

SERVES 1

Tajin, for rim (optional)

3 large basil leaves for mental clarity

¼ ounce agave

⅛ teaspoon ground cayenne for hex-breaking

⅛ teaspoon ground turmeric for purification

2 slices fresh ginger for success and power

½ ounce freshly squeezed lime juice for hex-breaking

2 ounces freshly squeezed orange juice for luck and blessings

½ ounce Lyre's Orange Sec (optional)

1 ounce Lyre's Agave Blanco (optional)

1–1½ ounces soda water or nonalcoholic sparkling white wine

Orange peel spritz, for garnish

1 Rim the glass with Tajin, if desired.

2 In your shaker, place the basil and agave. Sprinkle the cayenne and turmeric for vitality and purification and add the ginger for success. Muddle, stamping out any blockages or obstacles in your way.

3 Add the lime juice to cleanse limitations and the orange juice to uplift and inspire energy. Add ice, any nonalcoholic spirits, if using, and shake. Using the momentum of shaking to raise energy, say any intention or affirmations now.

4 Pour into your rimmed glass and top with soda water.

5 Garnish to invigorate your senses upon each sip.

BEYOND THE GLASS

In mixology, we often use a citrus twist as garnish: By spritzing the oils in the citrus peel onto the top of the drink and wiping it around the rim, this adds a lovely fresh citrus element that elevates the senses. This is also a great way to awaken your energy with magical mandarin, orange, lime, or lemon essence. To bless your energy with success when encountering roadblocks, take a citrus peel and squeeze it with intention while thinking on infusing your aura with that energy.

AFFIRMATIONS TO SIP BY:
I am wise in managing my finances.
Longevity flows through my financial resources.
My money supports my aspirations.

SPICED PEAR AMARETTO SOUR

Money, Longevity, Wisdom, Abundance

Sip in wisdom in money with this pear, almond, sage, and black tea spiced amaretto. Abundance is all well and good, but when not balanced with discernment, it can only go so far. This mystical mocktail is inspired by longevity and wisdom in money management so your funds can go further. Pear and maple are associated with both longevity and money, while clove brings in riches. Almond—the central flavor—resonates with themes of prosperity and success. Optional egg white clears energy, furthered by sage for longevity, wisdom, and focus. Altogether, this sip is associated with not just enduring abundance but also acuity. Sip while planning out your financial goals or casting long-lasting money magic spells, such as a maple jar (just like a honey jar, but with maple). For a spritzer option, forego the egg white, pour over ice, and top with ginger beer. If not using nonalcoholic amaretto, you may want to double the rest of the recipe.

SERVES 1

2 slices pear for longevity and money

2 leaves fresh sage for longevity, wisdom, and focus

¼ ounce maple syrup for longevity and money

Pinch of ground clove for riches

Drop of vanilla extract for money

½ ounce freshly squeezed lemon juice

1½ ounces nonalcoholic amaretto spirit or ⅛ teaspoon almond extract for money, prosperity, and wisdom

1 ounce black tea

Sage sprig, for garnish

Egg white (optional) for cleansing

1. In your shaker, place the pear and sage for longevity and wisdom. Add the maple syrup to bolster this energy, then lightly muddle.
2. Sprinkle in the clove as though raining down riches. Add the vanilla, lemon juice, nonalcoholic almond spirit, and any replacements, and black tea.
3. If adding egg white, shake first without ice. Then add ice and shake again.
4. Strain into a coupe and garnish.

BEYOND THE GLASS

Golden/yellow tiger eye is a stone of luck and good fortune. But it is also a stone used to enhance will power, protection, and the development of discernment. With its corresponding color but also themes of wisdom, it is a perfect match for not just good luck in finances but developing wisdom around them. Hold the stone while sipping on this recipe, pondering how you can expand your financial knowledge.

AFFIRMATIONS TO SIP BY:

Abundance is all around.

I am in alignment with my desires.

I effortlessly attract prosperity.

ABUNDANCE APPLETINI

Abundance, Money, Love, Healing

Call in abundance with the magic of apple, cinnamon, and bay leaf in this golden no-alcohol appletini. This lightly sweet, spiced beverage emphasizes the manifestation magic of apple—a symbol of abundance, healing, love, and magic in general. Complemented with its natural pairings of cinnamon, clove, and nutmeg, each sip invites luck and prosperity. Crowned with a bay leaf for success, this enticing drink will draw your desires to you in no time.

SERVES 1

1 teaspoon apple cider vinegar

1 slice apple

1 ounce Honey Syrup (page 199 in the appendix)

Pinch of cinnamon for success and luck

Pinch of clove for money and riches

Pinch of nutmeg for luck and money

1 fresh bay leaf for success and wishes

3 ounces apple juice for fertility and magic

1 ounce freshly squeezed lemon juice

Cinnamon stick or 3 additional apple slices, for garnish

1. In your shaker, add the apple cider vinegar to cleanse and neutralize any blockages to your abundance. Add the apple, thinking on its symbolism as mentioned below.
2. Add the sweetener for attraction. Then sprinkle in the spices, raining down blessings: cinnamon for fast luck, clove for riches, nutmeg for wishes.
3. Hold the bay leaf, thinking on your intention. Say any affirmation aloud now and then add it to the shaker.
4. Muddle these ingredients together. Then add the apple juice, lemon juice, and ice.
5. Shake, raising energy toward your intention.
6. Double strain into your prepared glass and garnish with a cinnamon stick for manifestation, or a fan of apple slices for an abundant snack.

BEYOND THE GLASS

From ciders to appletinis, apples make up some of the world's favorite drinks and dishes. And for good reason—this fruit is packed with magic and folklore. Apples are associated with love, healing, and fertility. When cut horizontally, the apple showcases a five-pointed star—a magical symbol associated with the five elements: wind, water, earth, air, and spirit. Altogether, it's a symbol of alignment between the classical elements to manifest. How can you invite alignment to manifest your intentions into the material plane?

AFFIRMATIONS TO SIP BY:

I am grounded in my body and trust in my knowledge.

My thoughts are clear and my mind is focused.

I work diligently toward my goals.

BLACKBERRY BLACK TEA BEVERAGE

Mental Acuity, Wisdom, Focus

Focus and get some work done with this sage and blackberry mint mocktail. This is the perfect sip to ground and clear the mind for productive energy. Mint helps hone the mind, while sage brings wisdom. Lavender invokes peace and melds with the luscious blackberry, while lime cleanses away unwanted distractions. Sip before studying or researching, or share over thoughtful conversation.

SERVES 1

5 mint leaves for mental abilities and calming

2 sage leaves for wisdom and focus

2–3 blackberries for healing and grounding

1½ ounces Honey Syrup (page 199 in the appendix) for spirituality and wisdom

6 dashes nonalcoholic lavender bitters (such as All The Bitter) for peace

1 ounce freshly squeezed lime juice

1½ ounces black tea for conscious mind and courage

1½–2 ounces grapefruit or plain soda water

Mint sprig, for garnish

1 In your shaker, place the mint for the mind, the sage for wisdom, the blackberries, and syrup. Muddle them together, as though muddling away any distractions and bringing your mind to the present moment through movement. Say any affirmations that resonate now.

2 Add the bitters, a perfect match for the blackberry and to uplift the mind. Add the lime juice, cleansing away any blockages to focus, and the tea.

3 Add ice, shake, and pour into a glass. Top with grapefruit soda water, its essence bringing positivity and the bubbles uplifting your energy.

4 For garnish, slap the mint sprig to bring out the oils and bring your mind to the present moment with each sip.

BEYOND THE GLASS

This drink contains the greens of mint, sage, and lime and the purples of blackberry and black tea. This color combo (and intention) perfectly matches the stone of focus: fluorite. Fluorite is known as a focusing stone, helping to clear the mind of clutter. In this way, fluorite helps soothe anxiety and worry. Altogether, it's a wonderful stone for students and for honing the mind! Hold it as you sip.

MANIFESTING with a SPRINKLE of SPICE

From pumpkin spice to curry and eggnog, spices have given flavor to the world. They enhance the aromas of what we eat and drink *but also* our spells: Cinnamon is a common ingredient in fast luck spells, and nutmeg is used in money charm bags or for fidelity. Spices are powerful ingredients in manifestation magic. And luckily, they are also amazing to add to drink recipes.

Spices are ingredients used for aromatizing and flavoring food. Often sold dried or ground, they are cultivated a variety of ways and ingrained in a history of trade throughout the world. Each spice has its own history, magic, and meaning, but in general they are all energetically warming and thus help raise spiritual energy or purify and enhance psychic powers. And since they are often already in your cabinets, they're great and easy ingredients to incorporate into your drinks and spells. Through using them with intentionality, and even relating the spices you use in your glass to your spells and rituals, you can manifest like a pro. Just remember that a little goes a long way!

IN MAGIC, YOU CAN:

- Use spices as candle dressing (sparingly, since they can also often spark very easily).
- Use them as powders to sprinkle symbols around a spell or candle.
- Add to charm bags as a talisman.
- Use in ground or whole form.
- Add them to simmer pots to aromatize the home.

IN MYSTICAL MOCKTAIL MIXOLOGY, YOU CAN:

- Use them mixed with sugar or salt as a rim to add magic to each sip.
- Mix them into attracting syrups, combining the alluring energy of sugar and spice.
- Sprinkle them into drinks, envisioning "raining down" a blessing or intention.

HERE ARE FIVE KEY SPICES FOR MANIFESTATION MAGIC AND HOW TO USE THEM:

ALLSPICE

Abundance, Courage, Healing, Luck, Money, Wealth

With a flavor that combines the essences of cinnamon, clove, nutmeg, and pepper, allspice is a multifaceted spice and magical ingredient. It is the unripe berry of the *Pimenta dioica* tree and available in dried berry or ground form. In magic, this versatile spice is primarily used for attracting money, luck, or healing. With its fiery energy combining the aroma of pepper with warming spices, it can also invoke a sense of power with which to conquer and succeed at goals.

CARDAMOM

Comfort, Mood-Boosting, Love, Lust

Cardamom adds a slightly sweet, spiced flavor with an edge of lemony-ness or minty-ness. This spice originated in India and is essential for favorites like the chai latte. In magic, cardamom is one of my favorite spices to use for adding loving, comforting energy. While it is often associated with lust (as it was once considered an aphrodisiac), cardamom has a warming and comforting energy that can bring love into any situation. Cardamom is available as "pods," small green fruit capsules, whereby seeds with densely packed oils are inside (hence its strength of power), or in a ground form. But be careful—too much and it can quickly become overwhelming.

CINNAMON

Fast Luck, Love, Lust, Psychic Abilities, Power, Success, Spirituality

Cinnamon is the inner bark of trees from the *Cinnamomum* genus. It is shaved off and then naturally curls into a stick form that's perfect for stirring drinks or as a manifestation wand. There are two main types: Ceylon (often considered "true cinnamon"), which is more expensive and harder to come by, and cassia, which is used most for baking and recipes, as it is less expensive. In magical practices, it is an empowering spice employed for raising vibrations and quickening manifestation, such as for fast luck or speeding up results. Its aroma can purify a space or heighten psychic abilities, and its warming essence invites love as well. A popular ritual is to blow cinnamon into your home through the front door on the first day of each month to bring abundance and financial wellness.

CLOVE

Comfort, Dispelling Negativity, Love, Money, Purification, Protection, Spirituality

Cloves are dried flower buds from *Syzygium aromaticum* in the Myrtaceae family of trees, native to Indonesia. They are available in dried form (which is perfect for poking into things, such as orange or citrus wheels) or in ground form. They are burned to purify a space and dispel negativity—in fact, cloves are often used to stop gossip in spells. They can help simulate one's psychic senses and attract love and wealth or riches. I also love to use them for their warming and comforting energy.

NUTMEG

Luck, Money, Health, Fidelity

Nutmeg is a seed of the fruit produced from the *Myristica* genus of trees, a dark evergreen tree. It is available in seed form (which can be great for charm bags) or ground. In magic, nutmeg is often used for good luck and money. It can be used to improve one's psychic awareness as well. Along with chile pepper, it can be used to promote fidelity in relationships but also strength in pursuing one's goals.

BLESSING MIMOSA BOMBS

Blessings, Happiness, Wishes

Cheers to some New Year's blessings with these bay leaf bubbly pomander mimosa bombs. By freezing zesty mandarin and blessing spices in spherical cubes with a bay leaf at the top, this is a fun way to not just enchant your drinks and keep your champagne cool but also bless your guests with good luck, success, and abundance for the New Year. This recipe combines several traditions and magical ingredients for the ultimate magic: gifting a mandarin or orange citrus for a good New Year, nonalcoholic champagne to celebrate the New Year, pomander balls to bring blessings and good luck, and even a bay leaf for a wishing spell.

This requires a spherical, silicone ice cube tray that creates 2-inch ice balls in diameter. Keep in mind that the amount per ball may depend on the size of your ice cube tray. You can vary the recipe based on how many drinks you want to make, but I have also broken it down per individual serving so that you can mix it straight in a glass and forego the freezing part, should you desire—it's just as delicious straight in the glass. Fresh bay leaves are often in a refrigerated herb section at your grocery store. Dealcoholized or alcohol-removed sparkling white wine may be hidden in your local store's wine shelf, or you can order it online.

AFFIRMATIONS TO SIP BY:

I am excited for all the blessings coming my way.

Success, happiness, and healing greet me in the New Year.

Abundant possibilities are available to me.

recipe continued on page 198

1 MIMOSA BALL

1½ ounces mandarin or orange juice for luck

Generous pinch of ground allspice for money, luck, and healing

Generous pinch of ground cloves for comfort, money, and stopping gossip

Generous pinch of ground cinnamon for success

½ ounce Honey Syrup (page 199 in the appendix)

1 fresh bay leaf per ice cube for wishes

1 whole clove per ice cube (optional)

2½+ ounces nonalcoholic prosecco for fertility and money

1 In a measuring cup, place the mandarin juice for New Year's blessings and to celebrate the rebirth of the sun.

2 Sprinkle the allspice for money and luck, the clove for riches and to stop gossip, and the cinnamon for spirituality, success, and fast luck. Stir in the syrup to sweeten and attract success to you.

3 Pour the mixture into a spherical ice cube mold. In the closed mold, each sphere should have a hole. For each, place a bay leaf stem through the hole for blessings. The stem should stick deep into the mold while leaving the leaf above; if not deep enough, the leaf might pop out while freezing. Add a whole clove, if using, to represent where the stem connects to the orange. Freeze overnight.

4 To serve, in a champagne glass, pour in the nonalcoholic sparkling white wine. Thinking on your intention, gently drop your mimosa "bomb" (bright, orange, and spherical, like the sun reborn at yule) into your glass. The moon-associated wine grapes bring abundance, money, and bubbles, raising your intentions up to the sky with excitement. The champagne will infuse with the ingredients as the ball melts, so the flavor will slowly start to come out.

BEYOND THE GLASS

The bay leaf is not just a garnish or purely decorative element to mimic a citrus leaf—it is also a spell. In magical practices, bay leaves are often used for wishes. While the drink itself will lend to a magical celebration with friends, when everyone is finished sipping, invite them to clean their bay leaf and then write a New Year's wish or intention on it with a Sharpie. They can keep it in their wallet, place it under their pillow into the New Year, or even burn it.

APPENDIXES

PREPARATIONS

THE CLASSICS

- **Simple Syrup:** Equal parts sugar to warm water.
- **Honey Syrup:** Equal parts honey to warm water.
- **Grenadine:** 1 cup pomegranate juice to ¼ cup sweetener, plus ½ teaspoon orange blossom/flower water. Warm for 10 minutes in a small pot over medium heat, bringing it to a gentle simmer but not boiling. Add in orange blossom water.

SPECIALIZED SYRUPS

- **Lavender-Agave Syrup:** Steep ½ teaspoon food-grade dried lavender in ¼ cup hot water for 5 minutes. Stir in ¼ cup agave.
- **Rose-Honey Syrup:** Steep 1 tablespoon dried rose petals in ⅓ cup hot water for 5–10 minutes. Stir in ⅓ cup honey.
- **Lemongrass Simple Syrup:** Bring 6 grams lemongrass to a boil in ½ cup water, then add ½ ounce sugar and simmer for 5–10 minutes
- **Jasmine Green Tea Syrup:** Steep 1 jasmine green tea bag in ¼ cup hot water for 5 minutes, then stir in ¼ cup sugar.

TEAS

Since teas are water-based, they can run the risk of becoming watery in a mixed mocktail. For this reason, some of these preparations use twice the amount of tea. For the length of time, defer to the minutes specified for steeping on your tea brand.

- **Chai Tea:** Steep 1 tea bag in ½ cup hot water for 5–10 minutes.
- **Chamomile Tea:** Steep 2 tablespoons chamomile in 1 cup hot water for 5 minutes.
- **Green Tea:** Steep 2 tea bags in 1 cup hot water for 2 minutes.
- **Hibiscus Tea:** Steep 2 teaspoons hibiscus in 1 cup hot water for 5 minutes.

- **Jasmine Green Tea:** Steep 2 tea bags in 1 cup hot water for 2 minutes.
- **Matcha:** Steep 1 teaspoon matcha powder in ½ cup hot water.
- **Butterfly Pea Flower Tea:** Steep 1 tablespoon butterfly pea flower in 1 cup hot water for 7–10 minutes.
- **Rose Tea:** Steep 1 tablespoon food-grade rose petals (or tea) in ½ cup hot water for 5–10 minutes.
- **White Tea:** Steep 2 tea bags in 1 cup hot water for 3–5 minutes.
- **Black Tea:** Steep 2 tea bags in 1 cup hot water for 3–5 minutes.
- **Earl Grey Tea:** Steep 2 tea bags in 1 cup hot water for 3–5 minutes.
- **Yerba Maté:** Steep 1 tablespoon Yerba Maté in 1 cup hot water for 5–10 minutes.

DRINKS BY SEASON, CELEBRATION, AND THE MOON

SPRING

- **Ostara/Spring/Vernal Equinox:** Cherry Blossom Beverage, Free-Spirited Lavender Limoncello, Yerba Maté Mocktail
- **Beltane:** Lunar Passion, Marriage Mocktail, Rose and Maple Frozen Daiquiri, Passionfire, Fairy Fun Mocktail
- **Spring Moons:** Cherry Blossom Beverage, Strawberry Fields, Flower Moon Mocktail, Clearing Cucumber and Coconut Gimlet, Jasmine Peace Potion

SUMMER

- **Summer Solstice/Litha:** Positivity Potion, Fairy Fun Mocktail, Summer Sun Sipper
- **Lughnasadh/Lammas:** Apple Harvest Tea, Abundant Blackberry Money Mocktail, Strawberry Balsamic Beverage, Mango and Mandarin Road-Opening Mocktail
- **Summer Moons:** Melon Moon Cooler, Raspberry Moon Soother, Moon Goddess Colada, Self-Love Papaya Potion, Sweet Peach Sans-gria, Compassion Concoction

FALL/AUTUMN

- **Mabon/Fall/Autumnal Equinox:** Rose and Rosemary London Fog, Abundance Appletini, Cosmo-cally Protected
- **Samhain:** Blood Moon Mimosa, Rose of Remembrance
- **Autumn Moons:** Blood Moon Mimosa, Apple Harvest Tea, Pumpkin Moon Mocktail

WINTER

- **Winter Solstice/Yule:** Restful Witch, Winter Wellness, Blessing Mimosa Bombs
- **Imbolc/Candlemas:** Zero-Proof Candlemas Cocktail, Renewing Yuzu Sour
- **Winter Moons:** Matcha Moon-tini, Rose and Rosemary London Fog, Yerba Maté Latte, Road-Opening Orange Toddy, Moon Metamorphosis, Warming White Wine

HERBOLOGY

Agave—Agave is associated with lust and love. With its unique life-death-rebirth cycle and its myth of having risen from the body of Mayahuel, it can be connected to rebirth.

Allspice—Allspice is associated with money, luck, and manifestation abundance. It is used to promote healing, and its fiery energy can encourage a sense of power or confidence.

Almond—Almond is associated with money, prosperity, and success. It is also used to promote wisdom and healing.

Aloe—A cousin to agave, aloe has spikes on its outer skin, which is great for protective energy, but a healing lives inside, used to soothe burns. It is also used for luck.

Apple—Apple is the result of harvest, trees that dig deep into the underworld. It is commonly used in love magic, for healing wisdom, and even for divination. In fact, when cut horizontally, its five-pointed star is a symbol of magic and the four classical elements, in addition to the spirit necessary for manifestation on the mundane plane.

Apricot—Apricot is associated with love and often used in both blossom and fruit form to attract and gain favor.

Avocado—In magic, avocado is associated with beauty and love. It is also a great source of healthy fats, omega 3, and vitamins C, E, K, and B6. It can also help stabilize blood sugar and help you feel fuller.[12]

Basil—Basil is associated with love, protection, mental clarity, and also banishing negative energy. Its scent can be used to soothe anger and invite affection.

Bay Leaf—Bay leaf is commonly used in wishing spells, but it has a multitude of other properties. It is associated with prophecy and psychic powers, purification, protection, strength, wisdom, and success.

Beet—Beet has lots of benefits and can help lower blood pressure and boost heart health. Its manganese and copper content can aid in metabolism, energy, and brain function. In magic, it is associated with Saturn and the earth element. Its magical uses include love, beauty, and strength.

Black Pepper—Black pepper is associated with protection and purification, commonly used for grounding work as well as dispelling unwanted energy.

Blackberry—This summer bountiful berry enhances the sensual, lusty, and healing energies. It is also associated with abundance, money, and connection with fairies. Its vines give it associations of protection.

Blueberry—Blueberry is primarily used for psychic protection in magic.

Butterfly Pea Flower—Butterfly pea flower changes color upon contact with acid (such as lemon). It is a great ingredient to connect to transformation and harness the power of alchemy. It brings energetic themes of happiness, spirituality, and feminine energy.

Cacao—Called the food of the gods, cacao can help one connect to and share love. It is also associated with money and prosperity and was once used as currency.

Calendula—In magic, calendula is associated with psychic powers, prophecy and dreams, luck, strength, and protection. It can be used in baths to promote a radiant aura. Medically, it might be used to treat wounds, as it is an antifungal, antimicrobial, anti-inflammatory, and more. It can help heal injuries.

Cardamom—Cardamom is associated with love magic but also adds comforting, warming energy. It may help with depression.

Chamomile—A go-to tea for bedtime, chamomile is a great herb for calming the mind and inducing peace. It is also associated with money and abundance, clear communication, love, and purification.

Cherry—Cherry enhances themes of love, happiness, and abundance. It can enhance divination, and tart cherry is also popularly used to help with sleep.

Chile Pepper—Chile pepper is used to heat up energy, whether for spicing up love and encouraging fidelity or breaking hexes.

Cinnamon—Cinnamon is a warming spice that invites love, manifestation, luck-raising vibrations, abundance, and more. It supports the warming of energy in the body by boosting metabolism and balancing blood sugar to regulate energy.

Clove—Clove is a powerful spiced used to attract riches and money, purify and protect from negative energy, raise spiritual vibrations and energy, and bring comfort and/or love.

Coconut—Coconut is associated with the moon and used for magical intentions, such as purification, protection, spirituality, and love. Coconut milk aids with energy levels and is great for the immune system with its antimicrobial and antioxidant properties. Comparatively, coconut water has much less fat and is 94% water, is full of electrolytes, and has relatively low calories and low sugar.

Coffee—Coffee imparts active energy to both our minds and our bodies and has even been used in some witchcraft practices for divination. It helps add that fiery flare of awakening and inspiration.

Cranberry—Cranberry is associated with protection, action, abundance, and love. It is packed with antioxidants, vitamins, and minerals and is often used to tackle urinary tract infections.

Cucumber—Cucumber is associated with healing, fertility, and beauty. It is used to cool energy, and its health benefits include lowering blood pressure and nutrients like potassium, magnesium, vitamins K and A, antioxidants, and lignans (phytonutrients) as well as added fiber and hydration.

Dill—Dill is associated with health, love and lust, money, sleep, and the home in modern Western magic. Nutrition-wise, dill has vitamins A and C, calcium, and iron and can help improve heart health.

Egg—Egg is used in witchcraft practices for cleansing and protection, a spiritual symbol of birthing something new.

Fig—Fig adds richness and inspires energetic potency for divination, sensuality, strength/energy, and abundance.

Ginger—Ginger is a power root that can inspire personal power, sensuality, and the movement of energy within the body. Ginger promotes circulation and the flow of both blood and energy. It can aid in manifesting success, power, or money, spicing up romance, or even boosting healing and purification.

Grapefruit—Grapefruit is primarily associated with purification, but it can also boost one's mood. It helps to boost the immune system and hydrate the skin, among other benefits.

Hibiscus—Hibiscus has antioxidants, which help protect the body from inflammation and oxidative stress. It may also help lower blood pressure and improve blood sugar regulation. In magic, it is associated with love, lust, and divination.

Honey—The hard work and cultivation of bees, the world's first-known sweetener is good for spirituality (especially goddess spirituality), happiness, purification, wisdom, love, healing, and more. Health-wise, it is an antioxidant, anti-inflammatory, antibacterial, antidiabetic, and more. It's also popular in beauty recipes for the skin.

Jasmine—Jasmine is a multifaceted flower, associated with love and attraction but also manifesting money, prophecy and prophetic dreams, and spiritual energy.

Lavender—Lavender, a known relaxant, helps purify the mind for peace and happiness, enhancing intuitive connection and allowing one's inspiration and ideas to flow through easily. In witchcraft, lavender shares a lot of themes with its uses in aromatherapy: peace, calm, and stress relief. But this also extends to communication, harmony, and attraction magic in modern witchcraft.

Lemon—Lemon is associated with cleansing and enhances elements of creativity, joy, longevity, love, and friendship.

Lime—In magical practices, lime is great for cleansing away hexes and getting energy moving. It can also make way for healing and love.

Maple—Associated with love, longevity, and money in magical folklore, maple syrup is also essentially a tree "blood" and can carry the grounding, wise energy of trees and forests.

Milk—In general, milk is associated with spirituality, the moon, love, and goddess worship. It was once an offering to the gods and has a nurturing energy.

Mint—Mint cleanses the mind, enhancing cognition, mental power, and psychic and divinatory abilities. It is also associated with communication, money, luck, love, and protection.

Nutmeg—Nutmeg helps add energies of luck, money, health, and fidelity. It is often used in both ground and full-seed form for luck charms.

Orange—In magical folklore, oranges are often associated with inspiration, luck, well-being, and abundance. They can invite creativity and bring blessings.

Pomegranate—With plentiful seeds, pomegranate is a symbol of abundance, fertility, and luck. It has a history of use as a magical ink or even as a replacement for blood in ritual. This fruit is also associated with the Greek goddess of the underworld, Persephone.

Rosemary—Rosemary is often used for clarity, cleansing energy, and the mind (for peace but also memory and focus).

Salt—Salt is often used in witchcraft for cleansing, protection, and grounding, and to represent the earth element.

Star Anise—Star anise adds the energetic potency of one's psychic abilities, purification, clarity, and spiritual wisdom.

Tomato—In magic, tomato is used in kitchen witchery for health, abundance, love, and protection. It has vitamins C and B, potassium, and antioxidants such as lycopene, helping to reduce inflammation and heart disease.

Turmeric—Turmeric is associated with creativity and is burned for purification. It also may have the ability to help improve mood and aid in detoxification.

Vanilla—Vanilla, an expensive spice, is associated with love and sensuality, the mind, peace, energy, and money.

Watermelon—Watermelon is associated with the moon and with healing.

Yuzu—Yuzu can help inspire rejuvenation and relaxation. Used in winter solstice baths, it inspires renewal and awakening. It may also be given as a gift of good luck and prosperity.

ENDNOTES

1 Barras, Colin. "World's Oldest Chocolate Was Made 5300 Years Ago—in a South American Rainforest." Science.org, American Association for the Advancement of Science, Oct. 29, 2018, www.science.org/content/article/world-s-oldest-chocolate-was-made-5300-years-ago-south-american-rainforest.

2 T. G. Powis, A. Cyphers, N. W. Gaikwad, L. Grivetti, & K. Cheong. "Cacao Use and the San Lorenzo Olmec," *Proc. Natl. Acad. Sci. U.S.A.* 108 (21): 8595–8600, https://doi.org/10.1073/pnas.1100620108 (2011).

3 McNeil, Cameron L., et al. *Chocolate in Mesoamerica: A Cultural History of Cacao.* University Press of Florida, 2009.

4 Jacobsen, Rowan, and Sam Rushton. *Wild Chocolate: Across the Americas in Search of Cacao's Soul.* Bloomsbury Publishing, 2024.

5 Sarreal, Julia J. S. *Yerba Mate: The Drink That Shaped a Nation.* University of California Press, 2023.

6 Hussain, S. M., A. F. Syeda, M. Alshammari, S. Alnasser, N. D. Alenzi, S. T. Alanazi, and K. Nandakumar. "Cognition Enhancing Effect of Rosemary (*Rosmarinus officinalis* L.) in Lab Animal Studies: A Systematic Review and Meta-analysis." *Braz. J. Med. Biol. Res.* 55 (2022): e11593. doi: 10.1590/1414-431X2021e11593. PMID: 35170682; PMCID: PMC8851910.

7 Bowdring, M. A., G. W. Rutledge, and J. J. Prochaska. "Advising Patients on the Use of Non-alcoholic Beverages That Mirror Alcohol." *Prev. Med. Rep.* 47 (2024): 102888. doi: 10.1016/j.pmedr.2024.102888. PMID: 39345357; PMCID: PMC11437911.

8 Gascoyne, Kevin, et al. *Tea: History, Terroirs, Varieties.* Firefly, 2018.

9 "What Do Cherry Blossoms Represent in Japanese Culture?" Japan Airlines website, www.jal.co.jp/ar/en/guide-to-japan/experiences/cherry-blossom/what-do-cherry-blossoms-represent/index.html#:~:text. The sakura's meaning is also a reminder that life is fleeting.

10 Ware, Megan. "12 Health Benefits of Avocado." *Medical News Today*, MediLexicon International, www.medicalnewstoday.com/articles/270406.

11 Gascoyne, Kevin, et al. *Tea: History, Terroirs, Varieties.* Firefly, 2018.

12 Ware, Megan. "12 Health Benefits of Avocado." *Medical News Today*, MediLexicon International, www.medicalnewstoday.com/articles/270406.

WORKS CITED

Barras, Colin. "World's Oldest Chocolate Was Made 5300 Years Ago—in a South American Rainforest." Science.org, American Association for the Advancement of Science, October 29, 2018, www.science.org/content/article/world-s-oldest-chocolate-was-made-5300-years-ago-south-american-rainforest.

Baschali, A., E. Tsakalidou, A. Kyriacou, N. Karavasiloglou, and A.-L. Matalas. "Traditional Low-Alcoholic and Non-alcoholic Fermented Beverages Consumed in European Countries: A Neglected Food Group." *Nutrition Research Reviews* 30, no. 1 (2017): 1–24. doi:10.1017/S0954422416000202.

Bowdring, M. A., G. W. Rutledge, and J. J. Prochaska. "Advising Patients on the Use of Non-alcoholic Beverages That Mirror Alcohol." *Preventative Medicine Report* 47 (2024): 102888. doi:10.1016/j.pmedr.2024.102888. PMID: 39345357; PMCID: PMC11437911.

"Cacao Powder: Health Benefits, Nutrients, Risks, and Usage." WebMD website, www.webmd.com/diet/health-benefits-cacao-powder.

"Chanoyu—Way of Tea: The Japanese Friendship Garden of Phoenix: Phoenix." JFGPHX, www.japanesefriendshipgarden.org/tea.

Cunningham, Scott. *Cunningham's Encyclopedia of Magical Herbs*. Woodbury, MN: Llewellyn, 1985.

Cunningham, Scott. *Cunningham's Encyclopedia of Wicca in the Kitchen*. Woodbury, MN: Llewellyn, 2013.

Escalante, A., D. R. López Soto, J. E. Velázquez Gutiérrez, M. Giles-Gómez, F. Bolívar, and A. López-Munguía. "Pulque, a Traditional Mexican Alcoholic Fermented Beverage: Historical, Microbiological, and Technical Aspects." *Frontiers in Microbiology* 7 (2016): 1026. doi:10.3389/fmicb.2016.01026. PMID: 27446061; PMCID: PMC4928461.

Forêt, Rosalee De la. *Alchemy of Herbs: Transform Everyday Ingredients into Foods and Remedies That Heal*. Carlsbad, CA: Hay House, 2017.

Gascoyne, Kevin, et al. *Tea: History, Terroirs, Varieties*. Buffalo, NY: Firefly, 2018.

Hussain, S. M., A. F. Syeda, M. Alshammari, S. Alnasser, N. D. Alenzi, S. T. Alanazi, and K. Nandakumar. "Cognition Enhancing Effect of Rosemary (*Rosmarinus officinalis* L.) in Lab Animal Studies: A Systematic Review and Meta-analysis." *Brazilian Journal of Medical and Biological Research* 55 (2022): e11593. doi:10.1590/1414-431X2021e11593. PMID: 35170682; PMCID: PMC8851910.

Jacobsen, Rowan, and Sam Rushton. *Wild Chocolate: Across the Americas in Search of Cacao's Soul*. New York: Bloomsbury, 2024.

Legrain, Leon. "Ur of the Chaldees." *Museum Bulletin*, www.penn.museum/sites/bulletin/2567/.

McNeil, Cameron L., et al. *Chocolate in Mesoamerica: A Cultural History of Cacao*. Gainesville: University Press of Florida, 2009.

Powis, T. G., A. Cyphers, N. W. Gaikwad, L. Grivetti, and K. Cheong. "Cacao Use and the San Lorenzo Olmec." *Proceedings of the National Academy of Sciences of the USA* 108, no. 21 (2011): 8595–8600. doi:10.1073/pnas.1100620108.

Samarghandian, S., T. Farkhondeh, and F. Samini. "Honey and Health: A Review of Recent Clinical Research." *Pharmacognosy Research* 9, no. 2 (2017): 121–27. doi:10.4103/0974-8490.204647. PMID: 28539734; PMCID: PMC5424551.

Sarreal, Julia J. S. *Yerba Mate: The Drink That Shaped a Nation*. Oakland: University of California Press, 2023.

ACKNOWLEDGMENTS

I want to start by thanking my amazing partner, Ryan. Your strength through your sobriety journey inspires and amazes me. I am beyond proud and forever grateful to live in a world beside you. From being my guinea pig for recipes and helping me with camera settings and action shots, to cooking nutritious meals to fuel me when I stay up late, this work was first and foremost not possible without you.

Thank you to my mother, Maria, and stepfather, Rolf. From your feedback on photography to shipping me kumquats and Babcia's yerba maté cups, you helped keep me going with your enthusiasm. And thank you, Babcia, for lending your yerba maté gourds and sharing with Ryan and me how you would use them back in Argentina. You helped me find inspiration when I was stuck, and I'm always amazed at the wisdom and stories you carry.

Thank you to my uncle, Janusz, for reminding me to take care of myself and for loving the Hibiscus-Lavender Iced Tea so much I decided to include it in this book. And a special thank you to my partner's mother, Cathy, for making sure Ryan and I got out of the house and didn't go stir-crazy.

My deepest gratitude to my sober coworkers from The Mystic Dream, and all the nonalcoholic sippers who ever sat at my bar top. Your interest in my earliest recipes back in 2016 prompted me to make nonalcoholic versions. Drinks are about connection and without you, I wouldn't have dived into making nonalcoholic drinks ten years ago.

Thank you to Kate Davids and ARC Literary for fine-tuning the initial vision and proposal, and to Katie Gould, Andrews McMeel, and Amber Lotus Publishing for believing in my vision—and in my photography! Wow! I still cannot believe I got to not only create recipes and write this book, but photograph them as well. And the attention to detail and design takes my breath away. This book has been a dream of mine to create, and your feedback, patience, and gentle, guiding hands made this possible.

NOTES

NOTES